COMPETITION LAW
&
THE ENVIRONMENT

To my brother

Jonathan Portwood

COMPETITION LAW

&

THE ENVIRONMENT

By Timothy Portwood

CAMERON MAY
LONDON

Published 1994 by Cameron May Ltd.

ISBN 1 874698 35 X

Printed by Watkiss Studios Ltd

ACKNOWLEDGEMENTS

I should like to express my gratitude to a large number of individuals who have assisted me in the writing of this book. In particular, I would like to mention Mr. Richard Port for helping me hunt down materials and who read much of the text in draft; Mrs. Karen Gay who did much of the early typing from manuscript; my father, Mr. Richard Portwood for his assistance in the latter stages of preparing the typescript; and Mr. Nick May who has provided inspiration and been patient during the process of writing. Finally I would like to mention Bristol University and in particular the Law Department headed by Professor Keith Stanton for their support.

Timothy Portwood
Bristol
October 1994

CONTENTS

PART I: *8*

Environmental Protection and Competition Law:

A statement of the problem Legal origins - Stockholm '72 - World Commission on Environment and Development - The Earth Summit - GATT & NAFTA - EC 5th Environmental Action Programme - Polluter pays - precautionary principle - rectification of damage at source.

PART II: *22*

GATT: A level playing field?

Economic view - internalization of costs - shifting comparative advantage - GATT and competition law - GATT and environmental protection - Articles I-XX - Technical barriers to trade - Sanitary and Phytosanitary measures - trade related intellectual property - dispute settlement - GATT and the WTO.

PART III: *54*

NAFTA: A step beyond the level playing field?

Principal issues - NAFTA environmental provisions - side agreement on environmental protection - obligations under the side agreement - institutions established under the side agreement - dispute resolution - public participation and transparency.

PART IV: *72*

The EC: Interactive integration?

The Action Programmes - EC competition policy - environmental law and workable competition - competition law and environmental protection - affecting individual action - structure of EC competition rules - agreements and collusion - export restrictions - price fixing - customer restrictions - exclusive purchase obligations - joint ventures - acceptable restrictions - selective distribution - Article 85(3) exemption - environmental protection as a reason for exemption under Article 85(3) - Positive and Negative requirements - European Commission's approach - Block exemptions - Article 86: abuse of a dominant position - Exclusionary behaviour - unfair competition - the Merger Regulation and environmental protection - state intervention - state aids, environmental protection and EC law - Article 92(2) and (3) - supervision of state aids.

PART V: *200*

Conclusions: Can the interlink work?

Index: *205*

Table of Cases & Legislation: *220*

I.

Environmental Protection & Competition Law

Part I

ENVIRONMENTAL PROTECTION AND COMPETITION LAW

1.1 LEGAL ORIGINS: INTRODUCTION

The International Community's understanding of its responsibilities towards the protection of the environment has, since 1972 at the latest, taken a particular shape. In the early stages, policies and action on the environment were mainly focused on the solution of particularly acute problems involving identified territories, property rights and people. To such problems, traditional approaches modelled on fault-based liability appeared both appropriate and effective. The Trail Smelter litigation was the paradigm.

By the late 1960's and the 1970's, however, there was a general recognition that the fault-based approach was inadequate to deal with the newly perceived global nature of effects to the environment. Climate changes, ozone depletion, diminution of bio-diversity etc. seriously threatened the ecological balance of the planet as a whole.

1.2 UNITED NATIONS CONFERENCE ON ENVIRONMENT AND DEVELOPMENT (UNCED), 1972 CONFERENCE IN STOCKHOLM

This new awareness and concern about the environment was crystallised at the 1972 Stockholm UN Conference. It did so by linking progress on environmental protection with progress in economic development. The Declaration made at that Conference established several principles intended to this need. Unfortunately, however, because of the political and economic implications of restricting industrial, agricultural and other developmental activities arising out of protecting the environment, from pollution and the conservation of resources, progress in substantiating this link after 1972 was slow. In particular, opposition came from developing countries whose incomes were declining and who saw this movement towards slowing economic development as a threat to their very existence. Not surprisingly, therefore, the developing countries' attempts to create a New International Economic Order in the 1970's made no reference to, and took little account of, the impacts of development on the environment.

The 1980's saw a change in pace. A number of strategies were premised upon the need to link environmental protection with economic development. By way of example, the World Charter for Nature, adopted by the UN General Assembly in 1982, sought optimal sustainable productivity of all resources coupled with conservation and protection.

1.3 THE WORLD COMMISSION ON ENVIRONMENT AND DEVELOPMENT

In 1987 the WCED brought these aims together under the umbrella of 'sustainable development'. In its report 'Our Common Future' the WCED defined sustainable development as 'development that meets the needs of the present without compromising the ability of future generations to meet their own needs'. The idea, therefore, is for the present generation to continue to develop economically but without prejudicing the ability of future generations both to develop according to their needs and to have an environment in which they can exist at the same level or quality as preceding generations. So it is, therefore, that sustainable development is linked to the notion of inter-generational equity.

The notion of sustainable development has been subject to a number of different definitions. The UNEP has added to the WCED definition that it requires 'the maintenance, rational use and enhancement of the natural resource base that underpins ecological resilience and economic growth' and 'implies progress towards international equity'.

So it was then, that prior to the UN Conference on Environment and Development held in Rio De Janeiro, Brazil from the 3rd to 14th June 1992, commonly known as the Earth Summit, growing concern over the state of the global environment was seen to have an influence over the regulation of both economic development and international trade. However, sustainable development is in theory a deceptively simple concept. In practice, its application is fraught with difficulty not least because of the considerable amount of crystal ball gazing that is necessary to assess whether what is considered as development today is found to have been environmentally destructive tomorrow.

The status of the sustainable development principleat international law remains ambiguous. There are various schools of thought who consider that even after Rio it cannot yet be said to be a norm of international law. Nevertheless most commentators believe that 'it is a notion around which legally significant expectations regarding environmental conduct have begun to crystallise'. Indeed, one writer, Handl, considers that it might in time even become a peremptory norm of international law (Jus Cogens). See 1 YIEL (1991), 25.

1.4 THE EARTH SUMMIT

The UNCED Summit at Rio finalised a Declaration which represents a delicate balance of policy goals supported by developed and developing countries. The balance struck at the Earth Summit clearly shows the tension between environmental protection and economic development. The Declaration sets out two groups of key principles. These are, on the one hand, public participation, the precautionary approach and the polluter pays maxim supported by developed countries and, on the other hand, the right to development, poverty alleviation and the recognition of common but differentiated responsibilities supported by the developing countries.

What is clear from the Earth Summit is that no government can plead ignorance to the challenges facing our planet. By embracing the notion of sustainable development governments can no longer follow the path to economic development without taking into account the consequences of such development on the environment. In light of this, it would appear largely an irrelevance whether the principal is one of hard or soft law.

1.5 GATT and NAFTA

From the trade point of view, agreements between States primarily concerned with the Regulation of trade have also begun to include provisions relating to the consequences on the environment of economic activity. Pressure appears to have come from environmentalists calling for changes in international trade rules to permit, inter alia, the use of trade restrictions to achieve environmental objectives. In the run up to the 1994 GATT, this pressure caused the GATT Contracting Parties to resurrect the hitherto dormant GATT Environment Working Group in 1991. Although originally drafted in 1947, long before environmental concerns emerged as an important policy issue, GATT recognises that governments may find it necessary to take certain measures indirectly related to the environment. For example, Articles XX(b) and (g) grant exemptions from GATT's obligations for measures which would otherwise be inconsistent with the GATT but which are 'necessary to protect human, animal or plant life or health', which are 'necessary to secure compliance with laws or regulations which are not inconsistent with the General Agreement' and which relate 'to the conservation of exhaustible natural resources if such measures are made effective in conjunction with restrictions on domestic production or consumption'. Similarly, the GATT Subsidies and Countervailing Measures Code and the GATT Technical Standards Code, both which resulted from the Tokyo Round of Multilateral Trade Negotiations in 1979, reflect the development of the environment as a policy concern. Both contain specific references to the protection of the environment.

Similarly, environmental issues have had a strong influence on regional trade initiatives. The North American Free Trade Agreement (NAFTA) signed by Mexico, Canada and the United States has numerous provisions dealing with environmental issues including a signed agreement specifically devoted to environmental protection. The Side Agreement is concerned with the establishment, maintenance and enforcement of domestic environmental law, increasing public participation in the law making and enforcement process, providing for dispute settlement for persistent patterns of failure to enforce domestic law and creating mechanisms for collaboration between the Parties. Trade sanctions may be used to enforce these provisions in limited circumstances. Significantly the Parties undertake their commercial objects 'in a manner consistent with environmental protection and conservation'. They agree to 'promote sustainable development' and 'to strengthen the development and enforcement of environmental laws and regulations'. Although the language used is hortatory, it expresses the parties' intentions to interlink international trade and economic development with environmental protection.

1.6 THE EUROPEAN COMMUNITY'S FIFTH ENVIRONMENTAL ACTION PROGRAMME

Whereas the Community's early policy and action on the environment were mainly focused on the solution of particular problems, the latest Fifth Environmental Action Programme embraces the principle of sustainable development in a positive and forthright manner. The Programme is not binding. Nevertheless, merely by entitling it 'Towards Sustainability', the Community has indicated the prominence which the notion of sustainable development is to take in its future policy.

Following the European Council's Declaration made in Dublin in June 1990 that 'the Community must use more effectively its position of moral, economic and political authority to advance international efforts to solve global problems and to promote sustainable development and respect for the global commons' the Fifth Environmental Action Programme has developed a new strategy for the environment and development. Numerous positive statements relating to the principle can be found in the document. One of the most transparent is:

'All human activity, economic and socio- cultural, either prospers or founders on the quality of the relationship between society and the natural world. Development is 'real' only if it improves the quality of life. ... In this context sustainable development ... entails preserving the overall balance and value of the natural capital stock, redefinition of short, medium and long term cost/benefit in valuation criteria and instruments to reflect the real socio-economic effects and values of consumption and conservation, and the equitable distribution and use of resources between nations and regions over the world as a whole. ... In more prosaic terms [sustainable development] has been defined by the admonition: 'Don't eat the seed corn which is needed to sow next year's crop'. Such a definition is useful in injecting an important dose of realism into the debate on sustainability. In practical terms, therefore, the concept of sustainability is ultimately linked very closely to a society's or region's prospects of continued development and success and, in the case of individual enterprise, even their profit and loss accounts'.

The Dublin Declaration stated that 'the environment is dependant on our collective actions; tomorrow's environment depends on how we act today'. The Fifth Action Programme on the environment discloses the Community's concern that many of the great environmental struggles will be won or lost during the 1990's.

Whilst the Fifth Environmental Action Programme is designed partly to stir up enthusiasm, such that the statements above may not be applied in practice with the same commitment, the general tenor of the Community's understanding of sustainable development is the need to link the mechanisms and regulation of economic development with the need to protect the environment. There are numerous ways in which this can be achieved. Fiscal incentives or disincentives can be used to affect society's and industry's choices of the goods they produce. Hard law in the form of trade regulation can be used to a similar end. The purpose of this book is to investigate the possibility of using the rules affecting the way that undertakings operate on their markets (competition law or anti-trust law) to achieve environmental objectives.

1.7 PRINCIPLES OF ENVIRONMENTAL PROTECTION

1.7.1 THE POLLUTER PAYS PRINCIPLE

The polluter pays principle has long been an aspect of international environmental policy in the developed countries. Its primary object is economic not environmental. It aims at the elimination of hidden subsidies which were granted whenever a manufacturer produces goods without having to pay for the pollution caused in so doing.

The OECD's definition of the principle is that the polluter should bear the expenses of carrying out measures required by public authorities to ensure that the environment is in 'an acceptable state' or 'in other words the cost of these measures should be reflected in the cost of goods and services which cause pollution in production and/or in consumption'. The consequences for the protection of the environment are that goods which cause pollution should cost more than competing goods which do not. Consumers should be attracted to the cheaper 'green' goods eventually driving the polluter out of business, or at the very least forcing him to change his ways. The consequences for competition are that by requiring companies to bear the 'real' costs of their production processes, a better allocation of resources will result. Clearly, therefore, the principle should be applied without discrimination and should not be accompanied by other subsidies which cause significant distortions in international trade and investment.

The polluter pays principle has been endorsed and adopted by OECD. The principle is not binding on Member States, which are free to determine how far it should be implemented in their respective territories.

The European Community has taken a positive stance. In its First Environmental Action Programme in 1973, the EC endorsed the principle and the EC Council issued a recommendation on the application of the polluter pays principle in 1974. The principle has been one of the bedrocks of the four subsequent Action Programmes. Further, Article 130r of the Treaty of Rome as amended by the 1986 Single European Act provided a legal basis for the application of the principle as part of the Community's environmental competence:

'Action by the community relating to the environment shall be based on the principles that preventive action should be taken, that environmental damage should as a priority be rectified at source and that the polluter should pay'.

In the European Community, therefore, since 1986 the principle has had legal force. The Treaty on European Union which came into force in November 1993, has continued to endorse the principle along similar lines.

The principle has been implemented in a number of ways using tax measures, charges, and liability provisions of national law. For example, in the UK, pollution charges have been imposed for water course discharges and pesticides and higher taxes have been imposed for leaded petrol.

In the developing world, however, the principle has not been widely accepted. For example, in the 1972 Stockholm Declaration, there is no reference to it; indeed, the converse is true. Principle 12 caused the developed States to help bear the additional costs of environmental protection measures taken by less developed States. Nevertheless, the 1992 UNCED Conference declared that the polluter should 'in principle' bear pollution costs 'with due regard to the public interest and without distorting international trade and investment'. Gradually, therefore, the principle is gaining significance at the international level. It represents an important strategy for controlling environmentally harmful activities. It emphasises responsibility for an undertaking's true economic costs. It has an important role both for environmental policy and in making markets more transparent.

1.7.2 THE PRECAUTIONARY PRINCIPLE

The precautionary principle is a measure of prevention rather than cure. In some circles it is known as the 'no harm' principle which requires that precautionary or preventive measures must be taken whenever a risk of harm to the environment is foreseeable. The principle suffers from the same criticism as that of sustainable development in that both rely upon the foreseeability of harm. Successful protection of the environment for the application of the precautionary principle rests, therefore, on the extent of knowledge at the time that the activities in question are carried out. Whilst it makes it possible to apply objective foreseeability through the concept of constructive knowledge rather than actual foresight in the undertaking in question, this does not address the basic criticism.

The principle frequently finds expression in obligations to carry out prior environmental impact assessment of projects which are likely to affect the environment. Examples in international treaties include Article 206 of 1982 UNCLOS; Article 4 of 1988 Convention for the Regulation of Antarctic Mineral Resources Activities; and the EC Council Directive 85/337 on Environmental Impact Assessment, OJ [1985] L175/40. In addition to such treaties, the World Bank requires prior environmental impact assessment of projects before making loans.

Whilst the existence of the precautionary principle and that of prior environmental impact assessment is beyond doubt, the kind of risk necessary to bring obligations of harm prevention into play is open to considerable debate. Some States assert they are not bound to act until there is clear and convincing scientific proof of actual or threatened harm. This approach makes no allowance therefore, for scientific uncertainty in matters of prediction. Other States adopt a more realistic approach taking into account that the question is one of prevention of foreseeable harm and not one of responsibility for actual harm. A lower threshold of proof is required. Notions of 'reasonable foreseeablility' or 'significant risk' allow for a more flexible approach. The Montreal Ozone Convention provides a good example of the application of this more flexible approach.

A stricter version of the precautionary approach is to reverse the burden of proof. In this form, it is impermissible to carry out an activity unless it can be shown that it will not cause unacceptable harm to the environment. This approach has been known to have been taken in some environmental treaties. For example the approach is found in the resolution suspending the disposal of low level radioactive waste at sea without the approval of the London Dumping Convention Consultative Parties; the suspension of industrial dumping in the Oslo Commission Area without prior justification to the Oslo Commission; and the moratorium on whaling.

Depending upon which approach is adopted, the effect on competition in any given market may be considerable. Undertakings may challenge a competitor's activities on the basis that its activities pose a foreseeable risk of harm to the environment and should therefore be stopped. Alternatively, where the burden of proof lies on the producer, the ability to innovate and to introduce new products onto the market will become more restricted. Markets will, therefore, become less competitive unless and until a true eco-industry is developed.

The precautionary principle, like the polluter pays principle, has since 1973 formed part of the European Community's environmental policy. When the Treaty of Rome was amended by the 1986 Single European Act, the new Article 130r gave the principle a legal base as quoted above. As has already been stated the Community has put the principle into practice through its Directive on Environmental Impact Assessment (85/337/EEC, OJ [1985] L175/40).

1.7.3 THE PRINCIPLE OF RECTIFICATION OF DAMAGE AT SOURCE

The concept of rectification of damage at source is one which does not figure highly at the level of international law. The obligations under customary international law as set down in the Trail Smelter litigation stress compensation rather than specific remedies. There is no obligation under customary international law for the victim of damage to use such compensation to rectify the environmental damage complained of. Further, only in the exceptional cases do treaties adopt a form of responsibility for damage which is placed directly on States. Liability is imposed, if at all, for the non-fulfilment of a State's international obligations for which the State is responsible. Examples include Articles 139 and 235 of the 1982 UNCLOS.

Further, environmental damage is frequently difficult to quantify. Clearly, whenever environmental damage is caused, compensation should include clean up costs, damaged limitation and possible reinstatement of the environment. Unfortunately, State practice and judicial precedent are too limited in this field to draw definite conclusions. Some treaties provide for reparation of this nature including the 1969 Brussels Convention on Civil Liability for Oil Pollution Damage, 1984 Protocol; the 1989 International Salvage Convention; Article 8 of the 1988 Convention for the Regulation of Antarctic Mineral Resource Activities. Further, a claim for reparation of this nature may be inferred from the Cosmos 954 claim, (1979) 18 ILM 902. In that case Canada did not recover its full costs of clean up of $14 million. It claimed $6 million and settled for $3 million.

In addition, there is considerable debate as to where the burden of proof should lie in environmental damage claims under customary international law. The International Law Commission is in the process of developing a new regime of international liability applicable to activities involving the risk of very considerable harm, or a higher than normal risk of less serious harm in its report 'International Liability for Injurious Consequences arising out of Acts not prohibited by International Law', UN Doc. A/CN.4/429 (1990). The main feature of this regime is a standard of strict liability for environmental injury, except in certain specified cases including harm caused intentionally by a third party and cases of armed conflict.

As stated above, however, these developments do not consider what the appropriate form of compensation and remedy should be. The rectification of pollution at source principle requires a specific remedy rather than compensation.

The EC has integrated the rectification of pollution at source principle into Article 130r of the Treaty of Rome. It therefore has legal force. Its most notable application has been by the ECJ in the Commission -v- Belgium, Case C-2/90, the Walloon import ban of foreign waste case. There the ECJ ruled that waste created in one area is different from the same type of waste created in another area on account of the need to apply the rectification of pollution at source principle to the treatment of such waste. A region's import ban on foreign waste was not, therefore, a discriminatory measure. The foreign waste was a different product from the home produced waste. Restrictions on the movement of such waste could, therefore, be justified if intended to protect the environment.

Some of the implications of the rectification of pollution at source principle for the environment are clear. Compensation for environmental damage should be applied by way of clean up where possible. Alternatively specific remedies may be provided. In this way the principle dovetails with that of sustainable development. The principle's implications for competition can be seen in the Walloon Waste Import Ban case. Products which cause pollution should be characterised not only by their physical attributes but also by applying the need for rectification of environmental damage at source. The free movement of such products throughout the Community may, therefore, be restricted without fear of offending the rule against discrimination. Further such characterisation of the product will mean that from the supply side at least it no longer competes with products from other territories and to that extent will be deprived the protection of the rules against anti-competitive agreements.

1.7.4 CONCLUSION

The various principles developed for the protection of the environment, including those of sustainable development, the polluter pays principle, the precautionary principle and the rectification of pollution at source principle, have considerable potential for affecting the way in which the rules of international trade and competition will be applied. Attention should be given to the way in which competition rules and the bedrocks of environmental protection interlink. Although, as the EC Commission's Fifth Environmental Action Programme states, a conflict is often perceived between environmental protection and economic competitiveness, a careful and planned application of the rules and principles relating to competition and environmental protection respectfully need not result in conflict, reduce competitiveness and further the destruction of the environment, but the converse: competition in the products of 'eco industry' should in theory achieve a high level of environmental protection.

The structure of the book follows the stages at which environmental protection and the rules of competition may interlink. The first stage is the development of a level playing field through harmonised definition, implementation and application of both the rules affecting free trade, and rules for the protection of the environment. This stage is exemplified by GATT. It is the lowest form of integration of the two policies. The next stage is exemplified by NAFTA and the Side Agreement on Environmental Protection takes the level playing field a stage further, and provides a structured framework for the resolution of trade-cum-environmental disputes. The third stage evidenced in the EC system is the possible use of competition rules as a means of environmental protection, whilst attempting as far as possible to maintain workable competition in all markets. The final stage which has an empirical example is where the rules of competition are sacrificed whenever environmental protection requires. This postulates an interventionist system driving markets along the 'eco-route'.

II.

GATT:
A level playing-field?

Part II

GATT: A LEVEL PLAYING FIELD

2.1 INTRODUCTION

Unlike legislation such as the Clayton Act in the United States of America, the Competition Act 1980 and the Restrictive Trade Practices Act 1976 in the United Kingdom, and Articles 85 and 86 EC (as amended by the TEU), GATT together with the incumbent WTO do not explicitly address competition. Instead they comprise trade agreements intended to liberalize trade movements between the signatory parties. Nevertheless, it can hardly be denied that the liberalization of trade movements by derestriction of trade barriers has a direct effect on competition. A level playing field of conditions between markets means that the market participants operate in the same legislative environment. This is not to say that all market conditions are or are intended to be levelled out by GATT. On the contrary, naturally occurring comparative advantages caused, for example, by ready access to raw materials or cheaper labour costs are not affected by GATT.

This link between competitiveness and competition on the one hand and liberalization of trade movements in the GATT system on the other is the principal reason for the inclusion of a part on GATT in this work. The level playing field idea can be seen as the first step on the road to the integration of competition law and environmental policy.

Turning to the question of environmental policy by way of preface, GATT is undeniably a trade agreement. As explained in more detail below, its origins have nothing to do with the protection of the environment. Even in the initial stages of the Uruguay Round of negotiations, environmental issues were not explicitly on the agenda. Nevertheless, there are a number of provisions in and since 1994 a number of agreements attendant to the principal measure which address environmental concerns.

If trade and competitiveness must take into account the effects on the environment which is the major premise on which this work stands, then the presence of such provisions and agreements in the

GATT system is not surprising. In short the level playing field for competition and trade must take account of the needs of the environment and of sustainability. Explaining how this is done in GATT is the purpose of this Part. The GATT system is criticized and a number of alternative models are suggested.

The GATT represented the first attempt by the international community at global harmonization of economic policies and from the outset was a framework of rules and principles for negotiating reductions in trade barriers in order to promote competition and trade. Reductions in tariffs negotiated under GATT auspices have contributed to rapid international economic growth in the last forty-seven years.

The principal purpose of GATT, therefore, is to counter national measures taken to restrict the movement of goods between the signatory states. How such measures are treated depends not on a pure economic analysis of their effects but on the economic and political aspirations and motives of the states concerned.

National measures taken for environmental purposes can and do have an effect on trade movements. They tend to fall into one of two categories: those which set product standards; and those which restrict, charge or ban imported products in order to address an explicit environmental concern relating to their production and not their content. The seat of production is situated outside the country of consumption. This second category is often referred to as Trade Related Environmental Measures or TREMs for short. Examples include the US embargo on tuna imports harvested by drift netting which endangers dolphins in open seas; rules governing the use of CFCs in the production of white goods etc. Restrictions on the import of products drawn from endangered species can also be seen as a kind of TREM.

Product standards are covered by the Agreement on Technical Barriers to Trade. In its original 1979 Tokyo version, the preamble to the Agreement stated:

"Recognizing that no country should be prevented from taking measures necessary to ensure the quality of its exports or for the protection of human, animal or plant life or health, of the environment, or for the prevention of deceptive practices, subject to the requirement that they are not applied in a manner which would constitute a means of arbitrary or unjustifiable discrimination between countries where the same conditions prevail or a disguised restriction on international trade."

In contrast to the TREM question, in issues concerning product standards the pollution to be controlled is either within the product imported (i.e., it is one of its constituents) or it is generated as a result of its domestic consumption. Domestic regulation has the effect of resolving environmental concerns on imported and home-produced products alike. The usual format of such rules is the imposition of an excise tax. The purpose is to equate domestic social and private costs. GATT and the Agreement on Technical Barriers to Trade do not forbid non-discriminatory standards, subject to the conditions provided in the Code. These conditions are described in more detail below.

2.2 THE ECONOMIC VIEW

From the point of view of economics a number of arguments can be put forward for the interaction of environmental costs in the drafting and implementation of a trade agreement designed to create a level playing of competitive conditions. Two main theories have often been advanced suggesting that there is a tension between environmental concerns and liberalized trade: first the internalization of pollution costs by the producing country; secondly, the need for unrestricted shifting of comparative advantage. Both theories can, however, be satisfied when TREMs are used for the purpose either of restricting the import of goods from producers who do not internalize their social (including environmental) costs or in circumstances where pollution is transfrontier.

2.2.1 INTERNALIZATION OF COSTS

Traditionally the environment is seen as performing three functions in society: it is a public consumption good in the sense that it provides aesthetic and recreation services for the public; it provides raw materials as inputs for production; and it is a receptacle for waste from production and consumption. Only in the second case, as a production input, has the environment been included in traditional trade and therefore competition theory. The other two factors have normally been seen as "free" goods, not included in the trade equation.

There is however a cost involved in these other two factors. Using the environment as a waste receptacle reduces its availability as an source of asthetic pleasure and recreation. There is a social cost to pollution - a cost of production which has traditionally been borne by society at large. This means that the price of the resulting product is too low if it is accepted that production should bear its full social cost. This latter premise is part and parcel of the welfare school of economics:

"World welfare is maximized if domestic and international prices fully reflect social costs of production and consumption for all states" (d'Arge, "Environmental Quality and International Trade", International Organization, 1972, p.430.

The result of failing to include this social cost in the price of goods is very similar to a tariff, although a tariff affects the price directly whereas social costs have an at the stage of production. In essence, the consumption of domestic production is much higher than it would be if costs were interalized and consequently the volume of production for export is reduced.

There has been a gradual recognition of the need to internalize social costs. Europe and the OECD countries have introduced the "polluter pays" principle which is intended to encourage the reflection of the full costs of pollution control or preventive measures in the costs of goods produced and marketed.

As can be seen, therefore, the internalization of costs will level out the trade and competition conditions between producers and therefore provides one way of linking free trade theory and environmental policy. If goods bear their full price taking into account the pollution caused by their production and consumption, there should be a shift to less polluting substitutes. The producers of the old product may well find that competition from the new substitute is too great and will either fail or have to switch production. This is not a distortion of competition. Rather it is levelling out the playing field from the environmental point of view. And there are of course beneficial effects for the environment.

2.2.2 SHIFTING COMPARATIVE ADVANTAGE

Comparative advantages occur where producers in one region have the benefit over producers of competing goods in another on account, for example, of easier access to raw materials, cheaper labour, or in the instant case, of less pollution intensive methods of production. The advantage therefore rests upon each nation's unique mix of environmental resources. Tariffs and quotas distort this natural or comparative advantage in that they discourage a natural shift of production from a pollution intensive plant or operation to a more environmentally friendly one. Siebert has written:

"As it would be absurd to compensate international disadvantage in endowments with labour, skills, capital and land by policy measures, we have to let environmental advantages rule in the long-run". (Trade and Environment, A Theoretical Enquiry, 1980).

If then a country introduces pollution controls but does not pass on the cost of these to the producer or the producer is protected from competition from less pollution intensive goods by way of charges or quotas on the latter, the original distortion on the market is ignored and the comparative advantage of the environmentally friendly substitutes is wiped out. The purpose of pollution control is to express the true social costs of production. If pollution control is not allowed to affect the market by way of quotas or charges on competing products, it loses its efficacy.

Three categories of TREMs can be identified. The first are trade measures which are intended to offset domestic pollution control charges. On the analysis above, such trade measures are not welcomed either by free traders or environmentalists.

Other more poignant arguments can be raised. In the developed-underdeveloped country dichotomy, developed countries tend to have expolited their environments over the period of industrialization with little attempt to internalize the costs of pollution. It does not really hang in the mouth of developed countries to turn now to their developing neighbours and say that they should not use their comparative advantage in for example waste assimilitive capacity for their own development. The argument is that the goals of economic efficiency and trade welfare require an unrestricted shifting of comparative advantage. Trade measures should not therefore be used to compensate for the cost increase and volume decrease effects of pollution control on production. In other words, pollution control should affect pollution unhindered. Trade measures should not be used to distort this process.

The second type of TREM is in fact a sub-category of the first but is different because of the particular circumstances involved. Where one country has already internalized its social (including environmental) production costs, trade measures should be available to prevent a shift of advantage to foreign producers who have not fully internalized their pollution costs. Otherwise, pollution control will increase the price of domestic goods to the benefit of imports which do not reflect their true social cost.

The obvious problem with this type of TREM is the monitoring of social cost internalization. Nevertheless the theoretical force of such measures is compelling.

A number of conditions would have to be attached to such TREMs to ensure that they are directed at the pertinent situation and do not distort trade and competition themselves. A failure to internalize should be identified according to objective and standard criteria which take into account the country's pollution assimilative capacity. Failure to take this capacity into account would distort the natural comparative advantage. Second there must be some mechanism likewise to charge or ban domestic production which has not internalized. Third the measure must not apply to all foreign production but only to that which has not internalized the social costs. This is the distinction from the first type of TREM. Finally there should be some means of facilitating foreign producers to comply with the internalization conditions. Otherwise the TREM would operate to the long-term advantage of domestic production which might in itself distort competitive and trade conditions.

Such measures would be likely to achieve their objective. Assuming that some form of tariff is used: consumers would shift their demand from the non-internalized good to the internalized one on account of the former's higher price (provided that the tariff is sufficient to off-set pollution control costs); domestic industry benefits in higher output and prices; the environment would benefit in that more environmentally friendly goods would be produced at the expense of pollution intensive ones. The internalizing and tariff setting government benefits in increased revenue which could be channelled back into pollution control projects etc.

Tariffs are not the only way in which this type of TREM can be implemented. Quotas or foreign product taxes would have similar effects. Tariffs may be more difficult to square with traditional trade rules.

The third category of TREMs addresses a different problem - namely transfrontier pollution. These measures may be applicable regardless of whether all countries have internalized social costs of production:

"Although it is necessary that each country implements its domestic environmental policies, problems of a global scale cannot be solved by the mere accumulation of domestic environmental policies by individual countries. For any country to discharge pollutants into the environment - common property of the whole planet - is an "extranational" diseconomy, just as the external diseconomy of a business in discharging pollutants is not reflected in its costs. When this happens, that country's activities tend to exceed the level that is most appropriate when external costs are internalized, and are apt to destroy the environment on a global scale." (Okita, OECD Environmental Challenges for the '80s, 1981).

The economist's rationale for trade measures designed to address transfrontier pollution is based on the notion that the environment is a factor of production. Trade can be explained by the principle of differing product or factor values. It is assumed that the factors of production are mobile. The environment as a factor of production is mobile when water or air pollution crosses borders and reduces another country's ability to use its environment as a factor of production or as a receptacle for waste.

Arguments can be made that in fact the environment is not mobile and that each country has a physical endowment of land, air and water, each of which can be used or has an assimilitive capacity for waste. Notwithstanding such arguments, there is no doubt that pollution does not respect boundaries and one country's pollution can have a deleterous effect on another's production or waste capacity. The GATT has recognised that:

"A share resource, such as a lake or the atmosphere, which is being polluted by foreign producers may give rise to restrictions on trade in the product of that process justifiable on grounds of the public interest in the importing country ... " (1971 Studies).

This analysis stresses the foreign process and ignores the presence of pollution in domestic production. TREMs designed to combat transfrontier or global pollution should take account of all sources of pollution, foreign and domestic. Otherwise, foreign production could be affected to the unnatural advantage of domestic production when the latter is equally or more a source of pollution.

Therefore the importing country should only charge or impose quotas on the exporter's products according to the actual amount of cross-border damage done to the importing country's environment. Whilst economic arguments can be raised, the happier analysis of this type of measure is in liability theory: you've damage my environment by so much and should pay equitably.

Out of these three types of TREMs two can be discerned as bearing some justification: namely those designed to target non-internalized producers when domestic producers are subject to pollution control; and those designed to target trans-frontier pollution.

2.3 GATT AND COMPETITION LAW

Before considering the environmental provisions in GATT and assessing whether they do achieve something of a level playing field which benefits both trade and the environment, a review of the interaction between GATT and domestic/regional competition laws is necessary. The premise to this section is of course that GATT is not explicitly a measure of competition law but is a free trade agreement.

That there is a link between trade measures and competition has long been undisputed. Indeed there have been calls that the two areas should be combined in a single international agreement which would replace existing trade laws such as anti-dumping and countervailing duty legislation and competition laws covering the behaviour of both private and public undertakings. In February 1992 for example, Sir Leon Brittan, the then EC Commissioner with special responsibility for Competition suggested that anti-trust (competition law) violations that distort international trade should be subject to GATT panels. Just as the internalization of social costs is seen as the raison d'etre for the interlink of the environmental policy and free trade rules so Sir Leon Brittan highlighted the absence or lack of use of domestic competition policy as another potential barrier to free trade. If a country does not enforce its competition rules - or if its rules are significantly different from those of its trading partners - the resulting anti-competitive behaviour can create barriers and distort international trade and competition. In essence, the basis of this need for free trade rules and competition rules is again the level playing field idea.

The following gives a few examples of why the international dimension to both trade and competition is necessary: market definition for market power of firm's can no longer be restricted to the domestic territory because a firm's activities in other territories will have an effect on its ability to act independently of its competitors, customers and suppliers. Yet the firm's ability to enhance power enjoyed in one territory by activities in another may be affected by the trade law system between the two territories. Other areas where trade and competition policy overlap or interconnect include buy-national policies; anti-dumping laws; intellectual property issues; the formulation and application of product standards (and therein environmental concerns); the activities of State-trading companies; subsidies and quanitative restrictions (again with an obvious link to environmental policy); and product liability rules (again with a link to environmental policy).

Attempts have been made to tackle the increasingly global problem of competition and trade by states unilaterally - using their own competition rules to control the behaviour of firms and governments operating outside their borders (for example ss. 301 and 337 of the US Trade Laws and the EC's Commercial Policy Instrument) -, bilaterally or regionally - by setting up a coordinated regime affecting the contratcing parties, such as the EC and NAFTA -, and multilaterally where the OECD (Organization for Economic Cooperation and Development) and the UNCTAD (United Nations Conference on Trade and Development) have been working on voluntary guidelines to ensure that the definition and implementation of competition rules do not operate as a barrier to trade for a number of decades. In 1976 for example the OECD adopted guidelines for multinational enterprises which included rules on restrictive practices (OECD, Guidelines for Multinational Enterprises, 1976). In 1980 UNCTAD's Conference on Restrictive Business Practices adopted a set of Multilaterally Agreed Equitable Principles and Rules for the Control of Restrictive Business Practices (UN Doc TD/RBP/10 (1980)), later adopted as a resolution by the General Assembly.

Turning to GATT itself, after World War II, there were proposals to create an International Trade Organization (ITO). Its Charter was intended to include a section dedicated to Commercial Policy (Art 34) and a section on Restrictive Business Practices (Arts. 46-54).

The ITO never came into existence. The GATT attempted to take over the role the ITO would have played in international affairs. GATT did not, however, include the measures on competition policy present in the draft ITO Charter. Nevertheless, by 1960, GATT contracting parties had begun addressing competition issues by for example adopting a decision that consultations could be held if a party felt that it had been harmed by the restrictive business practices of firms from another contracting party (See, GATT, BISD, 9th Supp. 171, 1961). The necessary consensus for a multilateral agreement to similar effect was, however, missing.

The Uruguay Round of GATT has not adopted an Agreement on Restrictive Business Practices and has therefore not followed Sir Leon's 1992 suggestions. Nevertheless, the need for some sort of institutionalized and international link is clear from Sir Leon's proposals which are outlined below.

He considered that the GATT system was a useful starting point for a "common international competition policy" on account of its pragmatism and tendency to meaningful rules and rule systems. Further, GATT's new dispute settlement procedure with its emphasis on reduction of delays, procedural improvements, the implementation of panel reports and other reforms streamlining the process, would be more amenable to competition law proceedings.

Sir Leon suggested in addition some innovations. Only governments can address the GATT or request a panel. Since competition law addresses the behaviour of legal and natural persons, it would be necessary for such persons to have the right to complain to the GATT about restrictive practices in other contracting states. Indeed, companies can suffer as a consequence of distorting subsidies given to competitors. This highlights the need for companies to have standing with the GATT system if it is to be used for the resolution of trade distortion by the application of competition policy.

Sir Leon does not advocate that companies should be the subject of proceedings under GATT. He wishes to retain the existing delimitation to contracting parties. Nevertheless, the EC experience gives ample evidence of ways in which states can be penalised for the anti-competitive behaviour of independent undertakings. Governments could be placed under an obligation to use their best endeavours to prevent or punish illegal anti-competitive behaviour of companies incorporated in their territory. "Best endeavours" would have to be defined in the agreement. If best endeavours have not been made, the government in question could be required to come before a GATT panel.

With regard to international mergers, Sir Leon's suggestion was that the GATT panel dispute settlement mechanisms could be used to provide a forum for discussion between competent national authorities particularly interested in a specific case. A basis of common rules on the appraisal of mergers could be developed as could a common commitment to enforcement.

All of the above of course is water under the bridge for the present. Nevertheless, it shows the very real need for interaction between competition policy and trade law and the international awareness of that need. The increased interaction of competition law (properly so called) and environmental policy outlined in the remainder of this work indicates that within the GATT system the level playing field idea is essential for both and by establishing such a playing field in the specific context of one of the concerns, positive repurcussions are felt in the other.

2.4 GATT AND ENVIRONMENTAL PROTECTION

Turning to the GATT system and by way of preview, there follows an analysis of the environmental provisions in GATT to assess which form of measure or justification is applied. It is found that in fact the GATT exceptions to the free trade principle are not organized on any theoretical footing. Instead, trade measures (tariffs, charges, taxes, quotas etc) are permitted according to their specific purpose and are subject to a number of common conditions, such as proportionality and the most-favoured nation principle.

The GATT embodies rules governing international trade providing a comprehensive regulatory framework for a wide range of governmental actions that affect trade both directly and indirectly. On 15 December 1993, 117 nations reached agreement at the end of over six years of negotiating in the Uruguay Round of the GATT. The package agreed includes the establishment of the World Trade Organization (WTO) envisaging a single institutional framework for the multilateral trading system encompassing the GATT (as modified by the Uruguay Round) and the agreements and arrangements concluded under its auspices.

Although the Uruguay Round was launched before environmental concerns gained the prominence they now enjoy on the policy agendas of numerous countries so that the relationship between trade and environmental measures was not included as a separate subject for negotiation, environmental concerns are addressed in a number of provisions in GATT itself and in the attendant agreements.

The WTO preamble includes direct references to the objective of sustainable development and to the need to protect and preserve the environment:

"Recognizing that their relations in the field of trade and economic endeavour should be conducted with a view to raising standards of living, ensuring full employment and a large and steadily growing volume of real income and effective demand, and expanding the production and trade in goods and services, while allowing for the optimal use of the world's resources in accordance with the objective of sustainable development, seeking both to protect and preserve the environment and enhance the means for doing so in a manner consistent with their respective needs and concerns at different levels of economic development ..."

Although the Preamble does not provide any specific right or obligation, it is important in providing guidance to countries regarding policy decisions not explicitly or clearly covered by GATT rules. It is significant that the WTO Preamble is oriented more towards environmental protection than its predecessor in the GATT which had no reference to sustainable development and referred to the "full use of the world's resources" rather than the "optimal use" thereof, which former version could have been read to encourage resource exploitation. The inclusion of the notion of sustainable development sheds a very different conservationist light upon the GATT and WTO as a whole.

Within GATT itself there are a number of provisions in which environmental policy has or may have relevance. These are analysed below before considering the main exceptions to the system in Article XX and then the more subject specific agreements negotiated at the Uruguay Round.

2.4.1 ARTICLES I AND III

Articles I and III set out fundamental non-discrimination obligations. Article I defines the most-favoured nation principle and Article III relates to the national treatment principle.

Both Articles refer to "like products". There is no definition of like product. The extent to which the environmental impact of a product and its production method are relevant factors in the definition of "likeness" is therefore unclear. The Preamble set out above can be used to argue that the differential impact of otherwise similar products on the environment and the right of countries to protect their environment in accordance with the principle of sustainable development should not be ignored. Disputes over the relevance of environmental concerns and the weight to be attached could be referred to the environmental dispute settlement process in which environmental experts could be called to assist.

2.4.2 ARTICLE II

Article II is entitled "Schedules of concessions". Under the Article, the contracting parties agree to limit their tariff rates and other conditions on designated imported items to negotiated levels. They are prohibited from imposing import surcharges or discriminatory conditions. There is an exception, however, allowing charges on imports if they are equivalent to domestic taxes imposed on either the "like" domestic products or materials used in the manufacture of the imported product. There is clearly an argument that this exception could be used for the legitimate imposition of fees on imports which posed an environmental hazard. The national treatment requirement explicit in the Article limits abuse of the exception for purely protectionist ends. Under the old GATT version of the Article, a GATT panel in 1987 interpreted it to allow countries to impose taxes on imports containing substances which were subject to domestic taxes on environmental grounds provided that the amount of hte tax was based on the quantity of that substance contained in the import (GATT Doc L/6175, 5 June 1987).

Again the same problem over the definition of "likeness" as experienced in Articles I and III occurs. Consequently it is not clear whether fees on imports produced by an environmentally damaging process are excepted from the rule.

2.4.3 ARTICLE VI

Article VI deals with dumping. Dumping is defined generally as selling in another country at less than the price in the exporting country. Countries may under the GATT code impose offsetting duties equal to the margin of dumping on imported products only if the imports cause or threaten "material injury" to a domestic industry.

The definition of dumping and the amount of offsetting duty are complex, although the general approach under the original code prior to the Uruguay Round was one of flexibility.

As explained throughout this work, one key to environmental protection is that the price of goods reflects their true cost, including the environmental and other social costs such as the scarcity of the resources used, environmental harm caused, pollution emitted, clean-up, waste produced etc. If environmental policy is to be integrated into the trade and competition framework, the assessment of cost, price and therefore dumping should reflect the true environmental costs.

The forumlae in the 1993 Final Act does not indicate how cost of production is to be defined. The opportunity to include a more environmentally relevant formula to include the value of the environmental resources used in production and the cost of damage to the environment (clean-up) by production of the product was therefore lost. In short the polluter pays principle has not explicitly been embraced by the trade rules. This may have been on account of difficulties in finding agreement on the assessment of the environmental cost of production.

2.4.4 ARTICLE X

Article X provides for the publication of laws and regulations related to international trade. These include measures affecting a product's sale, distribution, insurance, inspection, processing or use. Transparency was a key feature in the Uruguary Round of negotiations and in particular in the working out of the WTO's procedure. Again however the opportunity to include express reference to information about the environmental consequences and costs of a product was not seized.

2.4.5 ARTICLE XI

Article XI governs the elimination of quantitative restrictions on imports and exports. A number of exceptions are written into the text some of which are designed to protect the environment. The first of these provides for the exception of "export prohibitions or restrictions temporarily applied to prevent or relieve critical shortages of foodstuffs or other products essential to the exporting contracting party". Under the 1972 version, the reference to "other products essential to the exporting contracting party" was recognised as including export quotas designed to conserve exhaustible natural resources. Significantly, the importance of any given product was to be judged according to the particular country concerned. Because the merit of many environmental laws is specific to the conditions obtaining the state of enactment, this admission is of particular importance. It is hoped therefore that the existing approach will be carried over to the 1994 version. One problem however is over the need for a measure to be of a temporary nature. How this can be reconciled with the notion of exhaustible resources is not clear. Again it is hoped that a pragmatic approach will be adopted, and the definition of "temporary" will be tailored to the particular circumstances of the case in question.

The second exception is for "import and export prohibitions or restrictions necessary to the application of standards or regulations for the classification, grading or marketing of commodities in international trade." Whilst the original intent behind this provision was to protect agricultural products, there is no particular reason why, assuming that the pragmatism in other areas of GATT will apply here, the provision cannot be used to cover classification of goods related to their environmental impact. The language is broad enough to cover quotas limiting the production and sale of environmentally harmful products.

The next exemption refers to import restrictions on any agricultural or fisheries product "necessary" to the enforcement of governmental measures to restrict the domestic production of either the "like" product or products which use the imported product. The notion of "like" product may be wide enough to cover endangered species and scarce natural resources provided of course that the "necessity" requirement were met and the equivalent restrictions applied to domestic production.

It is well known that there is antagonism and concern against the use of this Article as a means of wide-spread protectionism. Its purpose is to make watertight and possible the working of necessary forms of internal control. The reference to "necessary" is important in this regard. Along the lines of the proportionality principle in the EC system, this means that any form of regulation which has an unduly restrictive effect on trade would be inconsistent with the Article.

Again it is unfortunate that the opportunity to draft into the Article specific exceptions for environmental protection was not taken. The language is clearly wide enough to permit of such use of the Article. Numerous potential disputes could thereby have been avoided.

2.4.6 ARTICLE XVI

This Article covers the use of subsidies to domestic and exported production by a contracting party. The rules provide that any subsidy given to a product which has the effect, directly or indirectly, of increasing exports or reducing imports of the product must be notified to the contracting parties of the extent and nature of the subsidy and the estimated effects of it on the quantity of the imports and exports into and out of the country concerned and the circumstances making subsidization necessary. The possibility of negotiating a reduction in the amount of subsidy is given to any contracting party which considers that the subsidy will seriously prejudice that other country's interests.

The scope of using the GATT subsidy system to further the protection of the environment is large. Many environmental policies take the form of subsidies in one form or another. Provided that there is general acceptance among the contracting parties that environmental protection is a legitimate circumstance for the use of subsidies, the possibility of dispute will be reduced.

One amendment which might however assist in the furtherance of environmental protection would be to render subsidies imposed pursuant to a legitimate environmental policy non-contestable. The only area for dispute would then be to assess whether the object of the subsidy was truely for environmental protection. Again the environmental dispute panel assisted by experts could assist in the assessment of the factual matrix and characterisation of the subsidy.

2.4.7 ARTICLE XVIII

Article XVIII provides for the grant of tariff protection and other assistance by developing countries to promote the establishment of industries, provided it is consistent with "policies of economic development designed to raise the general standard of living of their people". This phrase is wide enough to encompass environmental policies and therefore could be seen a permitting developing countries to introduce measures of protection for domestic products when such products are consistent with the principles of sustainable development and environmental protection. Conversely the Article could be interpreted to forbid the use of trade restrictions for environmentally damaging industrial development.

2.4.8 ARTICLE XX

Article XX provides for a number of general exceptions to the trade rules. It is the most frequently cited reference when the GATT and environmental concerns are discussed. The Article refers, inter alia, to measures:

"(b)necessary to protect human, animal or plant life or health; ...

(g)relating to the conservation of exhaustible natural resources if such measures are made effective in conjunction with restrictions on domestic production or consumption; ..."

The exceptions are subject to two requirements designed to guard against abuse for protectionist purposes: the measures must not constitute a disguised restriction on trade and must not constitute arbitrary or unjustifiable discrimination between countries where the same conditions previal.

Looking to the legislative history of the provision, the first point to notice is that the word "environment" is not mentioned. Indeed when the Article was drafted in 1947 environmental protection was not per se a public issue. In short the Article was not drafted as a measure of environmental policy. (See Charnovitz, Exploring the Environmental Exceptions in GATT Article XX, (1990) Journal of World Trade 38).

The language of the Article is vague. Whilst there is scope for arguing that notwithstanding the draftsmen's intent, Article XX does permit some measures of environmental protection to be exempt from the GATT disciplines, it is clear that not all measures designed to protect the environment are covered and equally the question as to which measures are included is unclear.

The next point to note is that the Article will come into play whenever a national measure imposes a tariff or quota, denies national treatment or otherwise infringes a benefit accorded to another GATT contracting party (breach of the most-favoured nation principle). The scope is therefore broad and will cover most TREMs.

Because the scope of measures covered by the exception is broad it is fair and accurate to expect that the exemptions will be construed narrowly. General social, economic or environmental policies will not be legitimate reasons for the maintenance of a system of import quotas. The justification must fall on all fours with one of the exceptions in Article XX. Where a measure comprises a number of elements some or each of which infringes a GATT discipline, each infringing element must fall within one of the exceptions (i.e., have a legitimate justification) for the measure as a whole to be exempt.

A standard procedure has been adopted for the application of the Article: first there must be finding that the national measure or some part of it is inconsistent with the GATT. The infringing elements are then tested against the exceptions to see if each is legitimate. If so, the infringing element is then tested against the two conditions of no disguised restriction on trade and no arbitrary discrimination.

Turning to Article XX(b) - measures necessary to protect human, animal or plant life or health - although the language is broad and could cover both product standards and processes, the legislative history suggests that the exception is limited to the former. The drafters' intent was to exclude "quarantine and other sanitary regulations". This has been reinforced by the Agreement on Technical Barriers to Trade which adopts the same language but adds "of the environment" when referring to product standards. Under the rules of interpretation in the Vienna Convention on the Law of Treaties of 23 May 1969, both this subsequent Agreement made under the auspices of the GATT and the legislative history should be referred to when as in this case the language of a provision is ambiguous. Consequently, it is highly likely that Article XX(b) cannot be used to exempt TREMs relating to production processes from the GATT disciplines.

A further restriction which follows from the same approach to interpretation would be to limit the exception to domestic (as in national) perons, animals and plants since "quarantine and sanitary" measures are not applied to protect the health of people, animals or plants of other states. This restriction has however not been adopted by the recent Tuna-Dolphin Panel in June 1994 where the Panel could find no reason in the text or public international law to suggest why the derogation should be limited territorially. The Panel left unresolved the question as to what was the original intent of the drafters in 1947 of Article XX(b), finding, in consequence, that this was not relevant to today's interpretation of the provision. With regard to the question of scope, therefore, Article XX(b) was broad enough to cover the US embargoes on the imports of tuna and tuna products harvested in the easter tropical Pacific Ocean on the basis that the reason for the embargo was to protect the life and health of dolphins in those waters. The Panel went on to find, however, that the embargoes went beyond what was necessary to achieve the protection sought and therefore fell outside the meaning of the derogation.

If this approach to interpretation is correct, then it is Article XX(b) may be of some use for TREMs which are designed either to combat foreign transfrontier pollution or the protection of the global commons provided that they satisfy the "necessary" condition.

The second question when applying Article XX(b) is to test whether the measure for which the exception is being invoked and which is by definition inconsistent with the obligations under the GATT, is "necessary" to protect human, animal or plant life or health. In the Panel on S.337 of the US Tariff Act 1930, 7 November 1989, L/6439, it was found that in relation to Article XX(d) (which the Tuna-Dolphin Panel considered to have the same meaning as Article XX(b)):

"a contracting party cannot justify a measure inconsistent with another GATT provision as "necessary" in terms of Article XX(d) [and therefore (b)] if an alternative measure which it could reasonably be expected to employ and which is not inconsistent with other GATT provisions is available to it. By the same token, in cases where a measure consistent with other GATT provisions is not reasonably available, a contracting party is bound to use, among the measures reasonably available to it, that which entails the least degree of inconsistency with other GATT provisions".

The Tuna-Dolphin Panel in June 1994 summarized the definition as requiring that "no alternative exists" which is more in line with the GATT obligations of the contracting party. It went on to apply this interpretation to the United States tuna and tuna product embargoes and found that such embargoes would only achieve the purpose of protecting dolphins if other states adopted similar policies and rules. Since such a pre-condition was not inevitable (and indeed was unlikely) the Panel found that the embargoes were not "necessary" and indeed ran contrary to the objectives of the GATT system as a whole.

Article XX(g) gives more scope for the exception of TREMs from GATT disciplines. This covers measures "relating to the conservation of exhaustible natural resources if such measures are made in conjunction wiht restrictions on domestic production or consumption".

The legislative history of this Article is sparse. Practice suggests that the provision relates to both import and export restrictions (see First Tuna Products Panel, L/5198, 29 BISD, 22 February 1982). Secondly, all living creatures, provided that they are subject to consumption are "natural resources" (Ibid, and United States -

Restrictions on Imports of Tuna, June 1994). Further in the 1994 Tuna-Dolphin Decision, the Panel found that there was no reason either in GATT or in the general rules of international law why Article XX(g) could not include measures taken by a contracting party to protect an exhaustible natural resource located outside the territorial jurisdiction of that state.

Although there is no reference in (g) to a "necessary" link between the measure and the objective of conservation, one GATT Panel has ruled that a mere link of the trade measure to conservation is insufficient and that the measure must be one "primarily aimed" at conservation. This is further supported by the need for the measure to be made "in conjunction with restrictions on domestic production or consumption". (See Canada - Measures affecting exports of unprocessed herring and salmon, O/6268, 35 BISD, 22 March 1988). This reasoning has been adopted by the recent second Tuna-Dolphin Panel in June 1994.

With regard to the "domestic production or consumption" proviso, the GATT Panel in the first Tuna case ruled that the exception was not available because the United States did not have restrictions on domestic consumption of tuna and because its restrictions on production did not extend to every kind of tuna being barred from Canada. In the Herring and Salmon dispute, the Panel interpreted the proviso to mean that a trade measure had to be "primarily aimed at rendering effective" the domestic restrictions. In the Panel's view the Canadian measures did not fulfil this test.

A number of problems have been caused for the application of this exception by the latter Panel. First, no rationale was given for why it looked for trade measures to bolster domestic restrictions rather than for the trade and domestic measures to be complimentary as appears the test in the language of the sub-Article. This requirement makes the use of the exception for the protection of renewable resources difficult. Further it renders its use impossible when there is no domestic production to restrict - for example a ban on the import of an endangered species by a country to which such species is not indigenous. There would also be a problem when the product being restricted is different from the product being protected. An example can be found in the recent tuna/dolphin dispute where the restriction is placed on the import of tuna in order to protect dolphins.

Turning to that dispute, the Panel found that Article XX(g) could be used to exempt measures implementing policies, including conservation policies, within the enacting state's own jurisdiction. However the Article was found not to be wide enough to cover measures such as embargoes designed to force other contracting parties to change their own conservation (or other) policies. To decide otherwise would, in the words of the Panel, "seriously impair ... the balance of rights and obligations among contracting parties, in particular the right of access to markets". The United State's embargoes on tuna harvested by Mexico were found to have been aimed at changing Mexico's policies and therefore went beyond the scope of the exception in Article XX(g).

In conclusion, Article XX was not originally designed to protect the environment although its terminology has the scope to do so. A strict, black letter approach to construction would exclude many environmental measures. However the preamble to the WTO suggests that the narrow approach is no longer consistent with the agenda for the 1990s. Whilst a few issues do not fit in the framework, almost everything else to do with the environment relates either to the life or health of living organisms or to the conservation of exhaustible resources such as clean air, fossil fuels and stratospheric ozone. Nevertheless the risk remains that Article XX will continue to be applied narrowly and will be administered in a manner inconsistent with the increasing awareness of the need to protect the environment. If so, the need for a specific agreement on the protection of the environment and sustainable development within the GATT framework will increase.

2.5 THE AGREEMENTS ATTENDANT TO THE GATT

In addition to the specific provisions of the GATT there are a number of agreements which the contracting parties have signed under the GATT's auspices. Only those relating to the protection of the environment are discussed in outline below.

2.5.1 THE AGREEMENT ON TECHNICAL BARRIERS TO TRADE

The aim of this Agreement is to ensure that the use of mandatory technical regulations, voluntary standards and conformity assessment procedures do not create unnecessary barriers to trade. The increase in the use of such measures as product standards, labelling and environmental impact assessment in the contracting states for the purpose of environmental protection is undeniable.

The Agreement expressly recognises in words similar to Article XX(b) GATT that states should not be prevented from taking measures necessary to protect human, animal and plant life or health "or the environment". It goes further and indicates that each country has the right to set its own level of protection without the need to justify its choice. Contracting states are encouraged to adopt international standards where available, but there is no requirement for domestic standards to be harmonized.

Typically there are most favoured national and national treatment conditions attached to the application of standards to avoid discrimination. Further there is an obligation on governments to draft their standards in such a way that they are no more trade restrictive than necessary to meet their objective.

The Agreement does little to alter the content of its predecessor which came into force in 1980. The history of the earlier Agreement indicates that the new Agreement will be used to serve environmental purposes. Indeed since 1980, approximately 400 technical regulations with environmental implications were notified to GATT because the countries involved considered that they may have caused significant effects for trading partners. In fact none was challenged as being unnecessarily trade restrictive. This suggests that the Agreement will provide contracting governments with considerable latitude to combat environmental problems by way of product standards etc. without facing challenges from their trading partners.

The Agreement makes provision for transparency of policy making in the area of product and technical standards. In particular trade-related regulations on technical standards are to be published in draft form to allow interested parties to learn of legislative proposals, to submit questions and make inquiries. This is intended to assist governments and non-government organizations to react to environmental and other needs as effectively as possible. In this regard, much depends upon the will of the governments to react to NGO input.

2.5.2 THE AGREEMENT ON SANITARY AND PHYTOSANITARY MEASURES

This new Agreement has relevance for environmental protection in that it covers measures which protect animal and plant health, including that of wild flora and fauna. It also covers measures directed at the control of contaminants, toxins, disease-containing organisms and additives in human and animal food and measures to protect human health from pests or diseases carried by plants and animals. Where such measures take the form of technical standards or labelling, they will fall under the Technical Barriers to Trade Agreement.

Although states are free to take measures to protect human, animal and plant health, the Agreement provides that where such measures result in trade restrictions, they should be taken only to the extent necessary for health protection on the basis of scientific principles and evidence. Where such scientific evidence is lacking, states may take temporary precautionary measures while seeking further information.

The level of protection is to be chosen by the government in question on the basis of the risks involved. Again the Agreement encourages the use of international standards but is not aimed at the harmonization of domestic standards.

Again all sanitary and phytosanitary measures within the scope of the Agreement are subject to the non-discrimination conditions in the most-favoured nation and national treatment principles. However the measures may be adapted to the health situations of the exporting and importing states. Governments are required to adopt the least trade restrictive health measure possible to achieve the requisite level of health protection.

The transparency and notification obligations are similar to those in the Technical Barriers to Trade Agreement.

2.5.3 THE AGREEMENT ON TRADE RELATED INTELLECTUAL PROPERTY RIGHTS (TRIPS)

TRIPS is mentioned because of the definition of patentable subject matter in Article 27. Paragraphs 2 and 3 of that Article provide for exclusions from patentability. Paragraph 2 provides for the possibility of excluding inventions from patentability if preventing their commercial exploitation is considered necessary to avoid serious prejudice to the environment. Paragraph 3 allows governments to exclude "plants and animals other than microorganisms, and essentially biological processes for the production of plants or animals other than non-biological and microbiological processes". Plant varieties on the other hand must be protected by patents or some other effective system of protection or a combination of the two.

2.5.4 THE DECISION ON TRADE AND ENVIRONMENT

On the 15 December 1993 the Trade Negotiations Committee under the auspices of the GATT adopted a Decision on Trade and Environment. The purpose of this Decision is to draw up a programme of work to identify the relationship between trade measures and environmental measures to promote sustainable development and to make appropriate recommendations on whether any modifications of the provisions of the Multilateral Trading System are required. Specific reference in the latter proposal is made to: (a) the need to enhance positive interaction between trade and environment measures, for the promotion of sustainable development, with special consideration to the needs of developing countries; (b) the avoidance of protectionist trade measures and recognition of the need of the trading system to respond to environmental objectives; and (c) surveillance of trade measures used for environmental purposes, of trade related aspects of environmental measures which have significant trade effects, and of effective implementation of multilateral disciplines governing those measures.

As a result of the Decision, consultations are taking place to elaborate the work programme as defined in the text. The Decision is in effect no more than an agreement to look further into the problems of the interaction of trade and the environment. Nevertheless it does demonstrate a continuing recognition in the international community that development must take place on a sustainable footing and that the special needs of the developing countries should be taken into account.

2.6 DISPUTE SETTLEMENT

The Understanding on Rules and Procedures Governing the Settlement of Disputes sets out a new procedure for the resolution of dispute but has moved away from the more streamlined proposal in the Dunkel draft. Article XXII offers an informal settlement process which utilizes the GATT secretariat to provide its good offices. This informal process is likely to be successful in many environmental disputes. The exchange of information, data and explanations will often be sufficient to resolve differences between the disputants. Such sharing of information may also serve to promote both the harmonization of environmental standards and environmental protection. Using this provision, bilateral negotiations have been carried out for example between the United States and Mexico in relation to the tuna fishing and dolphin protection dispute. This process has resulted in a commitment by Mexico to introduce measures which make its tuna fishing methods more dolphin safe. The negotiations are on-going.

Where no such informal agreement can be reached, Article XXIII provides for the creation of a GATT panel. At present, the GATT panel will investigate the dispute and come to its decision. There is no requirement that this decision be adopted by GATT contracting parties. Consequently and by way of example the GATT Tuna-Dolphin decision handed in August 1991 has not been adopted by GATT contracting parties. The GATT decision strikes down certain provisions in the United States Marine Mammal Protection Act which are designed to protect dolphins from Mexican tuna harvesting methods. This dolphin protection law is widely supported by the American public, yet GATT contracting parties are now seeking to have the law deleted from United States statute books.

Under the new system each panel may seek information from any relevant source and may consult experts to obtain their opinion on certain aspects of the matter or dispute before them. This can apply to environmental experts in the event of a dispute involving TREMs. The informational source or experts have no right to be consulted.

In disputes involving factual issues of scientific or other matter raised by a party to a dispute, the panel seised may request an advisory report in writing from an expert review group. The review groups have no right to be consulted.

New working procedures for panels have also been drafted in Annex 3 to the Understanding. These allow a party to a dispute to disclose statements of its own position to the public and, at the request of a Member of the WTO, parties to the dispute may be required to provide a non-confidential summary of the information contained in their own submissions to the panel that could be disclosed to the public.

A major criticism of the Understanding from the environmental point of view, however, is the issue of public participation. The GATT system continues to limit public participation and generally requires hearings to be held in secret. This continued insularity goes against the trend in other international institutions which deal with environmental matters such as UNCED negotiations, International Whaling Commission deliberations, Biodiversity Convention and Climate Change Convention meetings. Indeed, such secrecy is only appropriate for matters of commercial confidentiality and national secrecy. The institutions mentioned have all succeeded in combining closed session meetings with a degree of public access. Public access will tend to improve WTO decisions by increasing their transparency and therefore public scrutiny over their procedures and decision making.

A second criticism is over the absence of NGO representation as an amicus in panel disputes. Not only would this increase the standard of debate and informational exchange but it would also increase the public legitimacy and democracy of the proceedings and therefore the decisions.

Finally, because the highly complex nature of environmental disputes with trade repurcussions, WTO decision making could be improved by the establishment of a special environmental dispute panel pool with panellists who have expertise in environmental protection and sustainable development policy areas. Complaining parties should be given the right to have one such expert panellist sitting on a panel seised of a dispute involving environmental issues.

In conclusion therefore the dispute process under GATT does encourage negotiations to resolve disputes. This step in the process may well be sufficient to dispose of the majority of disputes with environmental aspects. Where such negotiations fail the next step is the creation of a GATT panel to investigate the issues and give a decision. This decision must then be adopted by the GATT contracting parties before it binds the disputants. The process is slow and the absence of any automatic adoption of decisions means that they are often ineffective. This in itself may further distortions in the level playing field for both environmental protection and competition.

2.7 CONCLUSIONS ON THE GATT/WTO SYSTEM, COMPETITION AND ENVIRONMENTAL PROTECTION

As indicated at the beginning of this Part GATT/WTO is not a measure of competition policy. However, its free-trade regime is designed to create a level playing field in which the factors of production and resulting goods are free to move without discrimination in the national trade-related measures they face. By so doing, competition should be facilitated in that firms will have to compete on the basis principally of price to which comparative advantages will be pivotal.

The major criticism of the system is that it is far from perfect. The exceptions to the system including those for environmental measures are not economically based and therefore have a tendency to distort the natural shifing of comparative advantage. This means that the "natural" conditions of competition are distorted and there is a welfare loss in society at large.

Secondly, because the environmental exceptions are incomplete, the level playing field becomes distorted both at the expense of competition and free trade on the one hand and at cost to the environment on the other. Trade related measures taken for the protection of the environment must fit into one of the exceptions circumvented by non-discrimination and proportionality conditions. This may mean a watering down of the content of the environmental measure with a resulting loss to the environment.

Further the measure may be concerned with an some area of environmental protection which is not covered by the exceptions in Article XX GATT or one of the attendant Agreements. This means that governments must choose some form of protection other than trade related measures to achieve their environmental goals. When most environmental measures take the form of product standards, tariffs, taxes, charges or quotas, there is not much left in the armoury for the state to do.

Measures for the protection of natural resources are severely constrained by the need for there to be both domestic production and similar domestic measures to which the TREM is complementary. This means that TREMs cannot be used to protect resources in foreign parts when there is no counterpart in the legislating state. This may have a significant effect on the challengability of measures taken to combat transfrontier pollution and the pollution of global commons.

By failing to create a comprehensive and policy-oriented approach to TREMs, GATT threatens to distort the environmental playing field such that contracting states are not in a position to restrict imports of environmentally unfriendly goods when home production internalizes the environmental cost. This in turn has an effect on the level playing field for competition as foreign goods will, by definition, be cheaper than the home product, shifting the comparative advantage unnaturally and anti-competitively. The sum of this is to hinder the interaction of competition and environmental policy to the detriment of both.

GATT continues to operate in favour of free trade interests in developed states and supports unrestrained development of resources in developing countries. There are no explicit rules for the protection of the environment. This contrasts with the stance taken by the United States, Canada and Mexico when they negotiated the NAFTA committing themselves publicly to addressing environmental issues in both NAFTA itself and more significantly in a side agreement. Similarly contrast can be made with the EC Treaty as amended by the TEU in which environmental protection has been adopted as a specific policy area by the 12 Member States to be integrated into the definition and implementation of all other policy areas of the EC.

Similarly there are no specific provisions in GATT to combat the use of competition rules as a means of distorting the level playing field. This again contrasts with the EC. At the international level, therefore, the interaction of environmental policy and competition policy is at an embryonic stage if that. The main thrust of the rules is to create a level playing field for free trade. The levelling of the playing field requires that account be taken of the needs of the environment and that environmental costs of production be included in assessment of trade related measures to ensure that comparative advantages are defined properly and shift naturally. Similarly the level playing field requires that the content and application of competition law is standardized within the international community. Otherwise distortions will occur which may favour environmentally unfriendly products and producers to the detriment of environmental protection.

Following the successful conclusion of the Uruguay Round of negotiations, at the top of the list of the WTO's future concerns will be the interaction of environmental and trade policies and how to promote "sustainable development" and ecological well-being without resorting to protectionism. Protectionism would principally involve the use of product standards, process standards and/or pollution standards. Such regulations could work to the detiment of domestic producers in the face of foreign competitors not burdened by such stringent environmental legislation. The natural response is to seek to protect domestic industries by applying home standards to all products. Although with hindsight many industrialized countries would probably admit that this area of concern should have been tackled much earlier, the highly complex issues involved in the environmental-cum-trade debate could not have been adequately addressed in a Round so overloaded with other matters.

III.

NAFTA:
A step beyond the level playing-field?

Part 3

NAFTA: A STEP BEYOND THE LEVEL PLAYING FIELD?

3.1 INTRODUCTION

Another example of an inter-State Treaty framework designed to foster trade between the Member States is the North American Free Trade Agreement (NAFTA). The NAFTA is the first free trade agreement to address certain trade related aspects of domestic and international and environmental regulation and enforcement. Most significantly, in a side agreement on environmental cooperation the three parties to the agreement, the United States, Canada and Mexico addressed the problems created for free trade by disparities in the content and level of enforcement of domestic environmental law. The side agreement is particularly concerned with the establishment, maintenance, and enforcement of domestic environmental law in each of the parties' territories at similar levels, increasing public participation in the law making and enforcement process, providing for common dispute settlement for persistent patterns of failure to enforce domestic environmental law, and creating mechanisms for collaboration between the parties on environmental issues.

The NAFTA and the side agreement fall far short of the integration of economic and environmental policies found in the EC. It is not surprising, therefore, to find that neither the NAFTA nor the side agreement deal specifically with the enforcement and content of domestic competition law. Instead, both measures are designed to deal with the more basic and preliminary issue of the need to establish a level playing field in environmental law to prevent distortions to trade and therefore to competition. This Part outlines the environmental provisions in the NAFTA and the side agreement and attempts to explain first of all how the level playing field shall be created, and analyses the repercussions for domestic competition law.

3.2 PRINCIPAL ISSUES

The principal issues of the intersection between environmental law and free trade arising out of the NAFTA and the side agreement are:

(1) To what extent can trade sanctions be used as a means of enforcing international environmental obligations;

(2) Whether domestic and environmental product process standards should be applied to imported goods;

(3) What are the effects on trade and investment flows of different levels of national environmental regulation and enforcement between States;

(4) How might the effects in (3) be ameliorated and even negated;

(5) To what extent should environmental experts be involved in free trade dispute settlements.

Each of these 5 issues or questions go no further than answering the preliminary needs for there to be a level playing field in environmental regulation and enforcement for free trade and competition to flourish. Where there are disparities between the content and level of enforcement of environmental laws between States, producers in one State might find themselves at a disadvantage in relation to others, where the former producers have to include high environmental costs in the price of their goods.

The first issue above considers the possibility of using trade sanctions as a means of ensuring that States comply with their international environmental obligations. These obligations may arise from customary international law such as the principles declared in the Trail Smelter arbitration, [1939] 33 AJIL 182, or under international treaties to which the given State is a party. Using trade sanctions for such a purpose, however, may give rise to breaches of other international obligations, such as rules under the GATT. There are provisions found in the CITES [1973] 993 UNTS 243, and the Montreal Protocol on Substances that Deplete the Ozone Layer (1987) 26 ILM 1550 which fall within this problem.

The second issue concerns the application of domestic environmental standards to imported goods. Where such domestic standards differ between States the effect may be to impose a legislative ban on various imports. In the EC regime this is known as indirect discrimination. Clearly, the effect on trade will be most severe where the differences between various States' environmental rules are numerous and their enforcement against imported products widespread. It would seem that the only solution to such distortions on trade is to harmonise environmental standards between the States concerned. One question that this raises is whether the use of environmental standards in this way amounts to an unnecessary barrier to trade. The answer depends largely upon the priority given to environmental protection as against free trade. Where the concept of sustainable development requires certain environmental standards to be maintained, there is, it is submitted, a compelling argument that free trade sanctions should be used to prevent the import or export and sale of goods which fail to reach the required standard. Otherwise, the objective of sustainable development will be defeated by the very trade in the environmentally harmful product. One concern raised by environmentalists is that the creation of a level playing field will be at the lowest common denominator in both content and level of enforcement. This will be because States find themselves forced to lower their standards in order to compete. Such concern is misplaced. Provided that States can agree on a given level, there is no reason why such level cannot be at a higher rather than a lower standard. The only limiting factor will be the state of research and development in eco-products and industry of the given countries. The establishment of a level playing field must, of course, be accompanied by an effective system of supervision and enforcement between the States of the product standards. This concern formed part of the reasoning in the GATT Panel Report in United States - Restrictions on Imports of Tuna (1991) 30 ILN 1598.

The third and fourth issues focus on the existence of disparate levels of environmental standards and law enforcement between States. There are a number of concerns both for the protection of the environment and free trade. If disparate levels of both substance and enforcement of environmental laws between States are allowed to exist, this may lead to pollution havens to which undertakings are attracted by lower standards for their products and the consequential lower costs of production. The dangers for the environment of this happening are obvious. Further, the distortions to trade and competition are similarly obvious with the changes in trade and investment flows that would result.

The last issue focuses on the need to involve environmental experts in trade disputes. Their input is necessary to understand the effects on the environment in any given trade dispute. An example, where environmentalists were not deeply involved, is the Tuna case, which was criticised by environmentalists for the free reign given to '..... international bureaucrats' setting the substance of and enforcing international law.

3.3 PROVISIONS IN THE NAFTA RELATING TO THE ENVIRONMENT

One of the most important provisions for the protection of the environment in the NAFTA is its Preamble. This sets down a number of principles by which the commercial objectives of the agreement are to be achieved. Among these principles are three expressly concerned with the environment:

'Environmental protection and conservation ...

Sustainable development ....

Development and enforcement of environmental laws and regulations.'

Although the Preamble itself is hortatory and therefore not binding, the intention is similar to that found in Article 130r(2) of the EC Treaty (as amended by the TEU 1993). Free trade should only be developed if consistent with the protection of the environment. This is reinforced by the reference to the need to promote sustainable development.

The agreement contains what appears to be a hotch-potch of rights and obligations. This suggests that the parties' intentions were not to sculpture a comprehensive and exhaustive set of rights and duties relating to the protection of the environment. The principal aim behind the NAFTA is the regulation of free trade. The environmental concerns covered by the agreement are therefore closely related to trade issues.

The side agreement is where a more comprehensive set of procedural and enforcement rights relating to the environment are found. It appears that in the side agreement there is no specific need to link the environmental issue with trade related matters.

Within the NAFTA itself a number of principles are set out with regard to environmental issues. The first is found in Article 104. This grants a set of priorities by which the relationship between environmental and conservation agreements on the one hand, and free trade agreements on the other, is to be assessed. Cites, the Montreal Protocol on Substances that Deplete the Ozone Layer, and the Basle Convention on the Control of Transboundary Movements of Hazardous Wastes and their Disposal are given specific mention. Other environmental agreements are listed in the Annex to Article 104. Where there is conflict between the provisions in any of these environmental agreements and the NAFTA, the environmental agreement is to prevail.

This priority given to international environmental legal obligations is supported by a choice of forum rule for general dispute settlement. The dispute is to be tried under the NAFTA rather than under other dispute mechanisms. This preserves the priority structure in Article 104.

Where there is an inconsistency between the NAFTA and an environmental international obligation, the NAFTA party is obliged by Article 104(1) to choose the method of compliance with the environmental obligation which is least inconsistent with its obligations under the NAFTA. This is designed to prevent a party from using an environmental agreement to protect domestic production which is necessitated by the environmental agreement. Further, the environmental obligation should not be applied in a manner which would constitute a means of arbitrary or unjustifiable discrimination between States where the same obligations prevail or which would threaten to distort international trade.

The interpretation of this principle is obviously open to doubt. Some guidance may be taken from a decision by the GATT Panel in <u>Thailand-Restrictions on Importation of and Internal Taxes from Cigarettes</u> GATT, BISD37S/200. Here the Panel concluded that a measure could only be found to be 'necessary' under the then Article XX(b) if there was no alternative measure consistent with the GATT, or less inconsistent with it, which the Country implementing the measure could reasonably have expected to employ to achieve its health policy objectives.

Article 104 of the NAFTA operates in two ways. Firstly, it is designed to limit the distortions to free trade and therefore competition between the parties to the least interference necessary as required by the needs for the protection of the environment as defined by the parties' international obligations. On the other hand, it is also intended to ensure that free trade is not used as a means of interfering with the parties' national environmental obligations which authorise trade restrictions in certain instances. It should be remembered that such restrictions are pursuant to bilateral or multilateral agreements between States and are not the result of unilateral action. The Tuna dispute will not, therefore, be protected by Article 104. In that case the action concerned was unilateral, and therefore not part of the United States International obligations. Article 104 is not, therefore, a mandate to States unilaterally to erect barriers to trade by enacting a high level of environmental protection through domestic law and applying such rules to international trade flows.

It is to this issue, namely the application of domestic environmental standards to imported goods, that we now turn. NAFTA has a set of provisions which deals specifically with the unilateral setting of domestic standards for imported goods. With respect to technical standards generally, Article 904(2) provides that each party may, in pursuing its legitimate objectives, which include the environment, establish levels of protection that it considers appropriate. When setting such levels of protection, however, the party must follow the procedure set out in Article 907(2). This provides that the party must assess the risk and should avoid the imposition of unjustifiable distinctions between similar goods or services from other states.

Article 905(1) encourages each party to use international standards as a basis for its standard related measures. Nevertheless, parties may depart from international standards 'where such standards would be an ineffective or inappropriate means to fulfil its legitimate objective, for example, because of ... level of protection that the party considers appropriate'. Consequently, parties can deviate from international standards when setting domestic levels. This would particularly be the case where a party wishes to set a level of protection that would be higher than that set down in the relevant international standard.

The general flavour of NAFTA in relation to domestic standards is that they must have a verifiable scientific basis. This reflects the concern found in a number of international agreements that States must retain considerable flexibility over the content and application of standards of any nature, there must be some safeguards against abuse. Otherwise, standard setting can become an exercise in protecting domestic production. The best safeguard is generally considered to be found in the need for scientific verification of a standard.

The third and fourth concerns set out above focus on the existence of disparate levels of national environmental laws and enforcement. Such differences can have a direct effect on the competitiveness of undertakings and consequently on international trade and investment flows.

The main article which addresses this concern focuses in fact on investment. Article 114 (Environmental Measures) states that:

"1. Nothing in this chapter shall be construed to prevent a party from adopting, maintaining, or enforcing any measure, otherwise consistent with this Chapter (11) that it considers appropriate to ensure that investment activity in its territory is undertaking in a manner sensitive to environmental concerns."

"2. Parties recognise that it is inappropriate to encourage investment by relaxing domestic health, safety or environmental measures. Accordingly, a party should not waive or otherwise derogate from, or offer to waive or otherwise derogate from, such measures as an encouragement for the establishment, acquisition, expansion or intention in its territory of an investment or an investor. If a party considers that another party has offered such an encouragement, it may request consultations with the other party and the two parties shall consult with a view to avoiding any such encouragement."

The emphasis is, therefore, that it is inappropriate for the parties to relax their environmental protection standards for the sake of increasing their competitiveness through the encouragement of investment. Consequently, the NAFTA does not specifically address the issue of existing disparate levels of environmental protection. Instead, its aim is to maintain the status quo and to discourage lowering of the existing environmental standards.

It should be noted that the settlement process is one of consultation. There is no process upon which the parties must resolve their dispute should consultation fail. Further, the consultation processes between the two parties concerned are not on the basis of a tripartite attempt to level out differences between their environmental standards. However, the side agreement specifically addresses this issue.

There are a number of disparate provisions in NAFTA which have relevance for the environment. Article 1106 prohibits the imposition of certain performance requirements on investors. It contains, an exemption from the prohibition, however, in favour of requiring investments to use particular technology to meet generally applicable health, safety or environmental standards related measures. Nevertheless, it further provides that such requirements must not be applied in an arbitory or unjustified manner. Similarly, the chapter on intellectual property provides that, in certain circumstances, the parties may exclude inventions from patent ability if such an exclusion is necessary to protect, inter alia, human, animal or plant life or health or to avoid serious prejudice to the nature of the environment. Finally, in the chapter on general exceptions to the free trade obligation, chapter 21, the provisions of Article XX GATT are incorporated mutatis mutandis. Consequently, measures 'necessary to protect human, animal or plant life or health' are permitted.

In conclusion, the NAFTA contains specific exceptions to free trade on the basis of the needs of environmental protection. However, because the NAFTA is not intended to achieve a high level of integration of the parties, the emphasis is on 'negative integration' rather than 'positive integration'. This means that the provisions are designed to eliminate or prohibit restrictions on trade rather than to create substantive environmental policies. The environmental content of the NAFTA is therefore by way of exception to the rule.

The effects on the competition laws of the parties are therefore relatively minimal. The parties can find within the NAFTA bases for allowing agreements which restrict competition between undertakings which are acting in their territories when such agreements have beneficial effects for the environment and alter the trade patterns between their states. Nevertheless, this is not something subject to the express provisions of the NAFTA but is more an issue of the relevant domestic competition laws.

3.4 THE SIDE AGREEMENT ON ENVIRONMENTAL PROTECTION

The Side Agreement was announced by the three Governments on 30 August 1993. It was published after some slight amendments on the 14 September 1993. Its focus is primarily upon the need to encourage domestic environmental law enforcement and to create new institutional arrangements for cooperation on the environmental matters between the three parties. A number of vehicles to achieve better environmental enforcement are prescribed, including greater transparency, private access to domestic remedies, and a tripartite approach to certain trade related instances of persistent patterns of non-enforcement of environmental law. One main difference between the Side Agreement and the NAFTA is that the former is not specifically trade related. On the contrary, many of its provisions are environmental per se. Indeed, of the ten stipulated objectives in Article 1 of the side agreement, only two, namely the need to support the environmental goals and objectives of the NAFTA, and to avoid creating trade distortions or new trade barriers, refer specifically to trade. The remaining objectives are: to foster the protection and improvement of the environment of the Parties; promote sustainable development based on cooperation and mutually supportive environmental and economic policy; increase cooperation to better conserve, protect and enhance the environment; strengthen cooperation on the development and improvement of environmental laws, policies and practices; enhance compliance with and enforcement of environmental law; promote transparency and public participation in the development of environmental laws, regulations and policies; promote economically efficient and effective measures; and promote pollution - prevention policies.

The Agreement sets out a number of principal obligations which can be divided into two parts; general commitments, transparency, civil and administrative procedures and remedies on the one hand, and cooperation and provision of information on the other. The agreement then goes on to set its institutional structure with the establishment of a Council, Secretariat and Joint Public Advisory Committee. It then sets out a dispute settlement procedure for persistent patterns of non-enforcement of environmental law. Each of these is explained in turn below.

3.4.1 OBLIGATIONS UNDER THE SIDE AGREEMENT

The general obligations of the parties can be divided into four camps: establishment of levels of protection between the parties; transparency of information relating to the environment; civil and administrative procedures and remedies; and dispute settlement.

3.4.1.1 LEVELS OF PROTECTION

Article 3 sets down the intention of the parties to establish a high level of environmental protection with a continued commitment to improving its environmental laws and regulations. Each party is free to set down its own environmental laws provided that it achieves a high level of protection. Consequently, a balance is struck between total sovereignty over each party's power to legislate for itself and the need to establish a high level of environmental protection. This provision is not new. Indeed, Article 9 (6)(1) provides that the parties 'shall work jointly to enhance ... protection of ... the environment'. Where a party introduces an environmental measure which could materially affect the operation of the side agreement, however, certain notification obligations apply.

3.4.1.2 INFORMATIONAL OBLIGATIONS

The Side Agreement establishes certain transparency requirements relating to information on the environment and environmental protection. This includes information relating to the law making process and is intended to enable any interested party to learn as much as possible about the laws of the states concerned. Consequently each party is required to publish promptly or otherwise make available its laws, regulations, procedures and administrative rulings of general application which affect any matter covered by the Side Agreement. Further, opportunity should be given to interested parties to comment on any such laws, regulations and administrative rulings.

In addition, each party is obliged to notify the other parties of any proposed or actual environmental measure that it considers might materially affect the operation of the Side Agreement, or otherwise substantially affect the other parties' interests under the Agreement. In addition, any party is entitled to request another to provide information relating to its actual or proposed environmental measures, and the addressee of such request must provide such information promptly.

Further, the Agreement's institutions have powers to request that parties provide certain information relating to their environmental laws and proposals.

3.4.1.3 PROCEDURES AND REMEDIES

The uniform, impartial and reasonable administration of laws, regulations and procedures is gaining increasing importance as a means of obviating or minimising distortions to trade. The Side Agreement continues this trend. Article 5 requires each party effectively to enforce its environmental law through appropriate governmental action. A non-exhaustive list of what may constitute 'appropriate governmental action' is found in Article 5(1) and includes: (a) appointing and training inspectors; (b) monitoring compliance and investigating suspected violations, including on site inspections; (c) seeking assurances of voluntary compliance and compliance agreements; (d) publicly releasing non-compliance information; (e) issuing Bulletins or other periodic statements on enforcement procedures; (f) promoting environmental audit; (g) requiring record keeping and reporting; (h) providing or encouraging mediation and arbitration services; (i) using licenses, permits or authorization; (j) initiating, in a timely manner, judicial, quasi-judicial, or administrative proceedings to seek appropriate sanctions or remedies for violations of environmental laws and regulations; (k) providing for search, seizure or detection; or (l) issuing administrative orders, including orders of a preventative, curative or emergency nature.

In addition to governmental action, each party is required by Article 5(2) of the Side Agreement to ensure that judicial, quasi-judicial or administrative enforcement proceedings are available under its law to sanction or remedy violations of its environmental laws or regulations. When assessing sanctions and remedies, the parties must take into account the gravity of any violation, the economic benefit derived from the violation by the violator, the economic condition of the violator and other relevant factors (see Article 5(3)).

There are also provisions relating to private access to remedies. The Side Agreement adopts a minimum standards approach in Article 6(3). This Article defines private access to remedies by way of a non-exhaustive illustrative list. Included in this list are the following:

(a) the right to sue another person under the party's jurisdiction for damages;

(b) the right to seek sanctions or remedies such as monetary penalties, emergency closures or orders to mitigate the consequences of violations of its environmental laws and regulations;

(c) the right to request the competent authorities to take appropriate action to enforce that party's environmental laws and regulations in order to protect the environment or to avoid environmental harm;

(d) the right to seek injunctions where a person suffers, or may suffer, loss, damage or injury as a result of conduct by another person under that party's jurisdiction contrary to that party's environmental laws and regulations or from tortuous conduct.

Locus standi rules are permissable in terms of conferring such rights only upon 'persons with a legally recognised interest' as determined by the domestic law of the party concerned. Because the locus standi requirement refers to domestic law, no definition is given of 'interested person' in the Side Agreement.

Minimum standards are reflected in the need for judicial, quasi-judicial and administrative enforcement proceedings to be fair, open and equitable (Article 7(1)). Proceedings should comply with due process of law, be open to the public, entitle parties to proceedings to defend their position by way of production of evidence and argument. Further, such proceedings should not necessarily be complicated and should not entail unreasonable cost and time limits. Unnecessary delays should also be avoided. Further, Article 7(3) requires the party to the Side Agreement to provide judicial review proceedings insofar as these are available under general domestic law. Finally, all Tribunals should be impartial and independent.

3.4.1.4 RESOLUTION OF DISPUTES

The provisions in the Side Agreement relating to dispute resolution divide into two parts. One part concerns persistent patterns of failure by a party effectively to enforce its environmental laws. The other part concerns all other matters which may form the subject matter of a dispute.

Dispute settlement for persistent patterns of failure to enforce national environmental law is set out in Part 5 of the Side Agreement. The phrase 'persistent pattern' is defined in Article 45 to mean 'a sustained or recurring course of action or inaction beginning after the date of entry into force with the Agreement'. Article 45 goes on to protect a degree of discretion in the national authorities to determine which offenses to prosecute through the setting of priorities. This discretion is however not unfettered. It must be reasonably exercised.

The definition of environmental law is found in Article 45(2). This excludes codes of conduct and other non-binding guidelines. The test appears to be whether the primary purpose of a statute or regulation falls within one of the three broadly defined environmental categories:

(a) the prevention, abatement or control of the release, discharge or omission, of pollutants or environmental contaminants;

(b) the control of environmentally hazardous or toxic chemicals, substances, materials and wastes and the dissemination of information related thereto; or,

(c) the protection of wild flora or fauna, included endangered species, their habitat and specially protected and natural areas.

Exactly how the predominant object of a given statute is to be determined is left undefined. Finally, certain statutes or regulations are expressly excluded from the definition and in particular those relating to worker safety or health.

The process for dispute settlement relating to persistent patterns of failure to enforce environmental law is initiated by a request from a party for consultations regarding an alleged abuse. Third parties which have a substantial interest may participate. The aim of this consultation process is to resolve the dispute there and then.

Should the parties fail to resolve their dispute within 60 days of the request for consultations (or such other period as the disputing parties may agree) any one of the disputing parties may request a special session of the Council under Article 23(1). This must take place in 20 days. Technical advisors and experts may be called on to assist. The Council should consider whether any other agreement or arrangement applies to the issue. If so, the matter is to be referred to the relevant procedure.

If no other agreement or arrangement applies, the Council's procedures are determined by the subject matter of the dispute. The Council may on a two-thirds vote on the instigation of any of the consulting parties, convene an arbitral panel under Article 24(1). This power is however limited to situations where the persisted pattern of failure to enforce environmental law relates to a situation involving workplaces, firms, companies, or sectors that produce goods or produce services traded between the territories of the parties or, that compete, in the territory of the Party complained against with goods produced or services provided by persons of another party. In essence, this means that the dispute settlement is restricted to the interlink between environmental law and anti-trust and/or trade law.

There are specific rules relating to the qualifications of the arbitral panel. The panel has 180 days (unless the parties agree otherwise) after the last panel list has been selected to produce an initial report under Article 31(2). The parties then have 30 days in which to submit comments. The final report must be issued within 60 days after the presentation of the initial report, unless the disputing parties agree otherwise under Article 32.

If the panel finds there has been persistent failure, it must make recommendations for the resolution of the dispute. It is anticipated that this would take the form of an action plan. The contents of the action plan are to be determined either by the panel or by the parties themselves should they agree.

Failure to implement the action plan may lead to reconvening of the panel. If the panel decides that there has been failure to implement, it may impose monetary penalties. The requirements for the imposition of a monetary assessment are set out in Annex 34 to the Side Agreement. Such assessments are limited to no more than 20 million US dollars or its equivalent in the currency of the party complained against. The amount may be increased in subsequent years. Paragraph 2 of the Annex sets out the criteria which are to be applied when assessing the appropriate fine. These include the duration of the party's persistent pattern of failure effectively to enforce its environmental law; the level of enforcement that could reasonably be expected of a party giving its resource constraints; the reasons, if any, provided by the party for not fully implementing an action plan; efforts made by the party to begin remedying the pattern of non-enforcement after the final report of the panel; and any other relevant factors.

The money is paid into a fund and is spent at the direction of the Council under the Side Agreement. The object of such disbursements is the improvement or enhancement of the environment or environmental law enforcement in the party complained against. Failure to pay the monetary assessment may result in suspension of NAFTA benefits.

With relation to all other matters which may form the subject matter of a dispute, Article 20(1) obliges the parties to endeavour to agree on the interpretation and application of the Agreement. Parties may notify another party of possible violations of its environmental law and in so doing may provide to the party information relating to the matter. The notified party is then obliged to take appropriate steps in accordance with its law to enquire into the allegation and to respond.

Finally, the Council may assist parties regarding the interpretation or application of the agreement under Article 10(1)(d).

3.4.2 INSTITUTIONS ESTABLISHED UNDER THE SIDE AGREEMENT

The Side Agreement establishes three institutions. The Council is intended to serve as a forum for the discussion of environmental matters within the scope of the Agreement. Further, it is required to oversee the implementation of the Agreement and its extension. It has duties to interpret and apply the Agreement, to adopt an annual programme and budget and to promote and facilitate cooperation between the parties on environmental matters. The Council is also obliged to cooperate with the Free Trade Commission (FTC) to achieve the environmental goals and objectives of the NAFTA.

The second institutional body of the Side Agreement is the Secretariat. This aids the Council in the fulfilment of its functions. It is headed by an Executive Director who has considerable autonomy over his staff. The Secretariat is intended to be independent of the parties. His purpose is to provide technical, administrative and operational support to the Council and to any Committees and groups established by the Council (Article 11(5)). It also has the function of drafting the Council's annual programme and budget. It also has powers to prepare a report for the Council on any matter within the scope of the Annual Programmes so adopted by the Council.

Further, the Secretariat is empowered to receive complaints from any person or NGO of a party relating to alleged failures by that party to enforce its environmental law effectively. These are referred to as 'submissions'. Article 14(1) of the Agreement sets out various criteria which may be met for a submission to be admissible. These include language and evidential requirements and must be aimed primarily at promoting enforcement rather than harassing industry. The Secretariat has a discretion whether to act on submissions. In exercising this discretion Article 14(2) sets out various guidelines. These include whether:

(a) the submission alleges harm to the person or organisation making the submissions;

(b) the submission, alone, or in combination with other submissions, raises matters whose study would advance the goals of the agreement;

(c) private remedies available under the Party's laws have been pursued;

(d) a submission is drawn exclusively from mass media reports.

Where a submission is to be followed up, the relevant party must be notified and must be forwarded a copy of the submission and supporting documentation. The impugned party must advise whether the matter is currently subject to a pending proceeding thereby staying the follow of the submission and must give other information that the party considers relevant. The Secretariat must then decide whether the drawing up of a factual record is necessary under Article 15. For this the Secretariat requires a two-thirds majority vote by the Council. A factual record is intended to supplement the information produced by the parties concerned. This factual record is then submitted to the Council which may, on a two-thirds majority vote, make it publicly available. The purpose of this approach is not to come to a resolution but to put into the public domain issues of environmental law which fall within the scope of the Agreement.

The third body comprising the Commission of the Side Agreement is the Joint Advisory Committee. This consists of 15 members, each party selecting an equal number. It must convene at least once a year. Its purpose is to provide advice to the Council on any matter within the scope of the Agreement. It is also intended to provide relevant technical, scientific or other information to the Secretariat.

3.4.3 PUBLIC PARTICIPATION AND TRANSPARENCY

In addition to the possibility of public submissions under Article 14 of the Agreement, the Council has power to seek advice from NGO's or persons generally under Article 9(5). Further, the Secretariat may draw on information submitted by NGO's when performing its functions.

3.5 CONCLUSION

Clearly, the NAFTA and its Side Agreement suffer from the stage of integration reached by the contracting parties. Consequently, the relevance of both agreements to domestic competition law is somewhat remote and indirect. The main purpose behind the measures is to develop a level playing field both in the content and enforcement of environmental law. This should have benefits both for the protection of the environment where a high level of protection is achieved, and for free trade. As such, the Agreements can be seen as one step prior to the objectives of the EC Treaty. The difference, in essence, is one between negative integration (NAFTA) and positive integration (the EC).

This conclusion is not intended, of course, to denigrate the advances made by the NAFTA and the Side Agreement. As stated in the Government of Canada's Environmental Review of the Agreement:

'... the NAFTA establishes a new bench mark for environmentally sensitive international trade and economic relations. The environmental provisions of the [Side Agreement] ... go well beyond those of any previous free trade agreement.' (See North America Free Trade Agreement; Canadian Environmental Review, Canada. October 1992, at page 71).

IV.

THE EC
interactive integration?

Part 4

EC LAW: INTEGRATION?

4.1 INTRODUCTION

The intersection of environmental protection and competition law in the European Community referred to in passing in the first two chapters has its own peculiar shape largely because of the specific content of EC Environmental and Competition policies and the methods of monitoring and enforcement. In addition, the intersection works both ways. The regulation of environmental protection cannot, because of the principal objectives of the EC, operate in a vacuum divorced from the functioning of European markets and industries; similarly competition law cannot be applied without due regard being given to the effects on the environment of authorised competitive activity. So it is, therefore, that the rules developed for the protection of the environment may be used to assist the development of a competitive 'eco-industry' and the rules of competition law may be used as a means of enforcing and monitoring a high level of environmental protection.

EC Competition Policy is designed to ensure a level playing field for market participants wherever they may be within the EC borders. Perfect competition in which goods are homogeneous and participants atomistic is not the objective. Indeed, because there are no opportunities to change and therefore to compete, the supposed ideal of perfect competition is arguably the converse of the aim in which there is no real competition. A better description of the EC's policy is 'workable competition' in which markets are not allowed to become so concentrated that market power rests in the hands of just one or several undertakings and where the opportunities for small and medium sized enterprises ('SMEs') have equal opportunities to participate and compete in European markets with their larger and possibly stronger competitors.

The enforcement of EC competition law formally rests in the hands of the Commission, whose powers are set out in a number of implementing Regulations, the most important of which is Regulation 17 of 1962. That is the formal position. In fact, because the Commission lacks the resources and personnel even to monitor the tip of the iceberg of agreements made between undertakings within the EC and the activities of market power for firms, the true role of monitoring and enforcing the EC's competition rules rests in the hands of the undertakings themselves. The initiative is given to undertakings in two ways. Agreements between enterprises which contain restrictions on competition where the parties are sufficiently large and the agreement has the potential of effecting trade flows between Member States must be notified to the Commission if they are to be rendered enforceable in the national Courts. The same is the case for mergers and similar agreements. Secondly, enterprises have a right to make complaints to the Commission relating to the anti-competitive activities of other undertakings. Such complaints may be either formal or informal. If formal, the Commission must investigate, whereas there is no such obligation arising out of an informal complaint.

Clearly, therefore, there is scope for enhancing this initiative inherent in EC competition law given to undertakings and to use it for the purposes of environmental protection by pressurising firms to take the environmental consequences into account when operating and competing on their markets.

In the early stages of EC environmental policy, the emphasis was on regulation with the initiative for both new environmental protection measures and the enforcement of existing rules resting principally on the EC Commission. In its Fifth Environmental Action Programme the EC Commission has dubbed this the 'top down approach'. This policy meant that individuals, undertakings and lobby groups etcetera, had few if any rights to enforce environmental law. The burden of enforcement lies, therefore, with the Commission and national authorities. The Commission is, however, inadequate for this task. It lacks both the resources and personnel to properly investigate alleged violations of its environmental rules and, in contrast to competition law, does not have the backing of a series of enforcement powers along the lines of Regulation 17. Nor, does the Commission have environmental investigators. Its powers lie in Article 169EC which is directed at Member States rather than individuals and companies. The principal objective of Article 169 proceedings is to challenge the failure of Member States properly to implement community rules. Investigating and sanctioning the environmentally dangerous and damaging activities of individuals and companies are several times removed from this procedure. Although the Commission's enforcement under Article 169 has intensified over recent years in the field of environmental protection, the system does not address the real question.

Another problem in the implementation of Community environmental legislation is that the legislation aims at protecting general and not vested interests. Natural media such as air, water, nature, soil and sea have, in the past, been seen and treated as common goods. They cost nothing and it costs nothing to discharge pollution into them. Attempts to restrict this liberty have, therefore, faced considerable resistance. Typical criticism brands measures taken to enforce environmental policy as being excessive, bureaucratic, unnecessary or counter-productive. Further, environmental catastrophe such as Torrey Canyon, Bhopal, and Sandoz are the exception to the rule. Damage to the environment comes mainly from the cumulative effects of authorised activities rather than major disasters or identify instances of illegal pollution. The need for scrupulous monitoring, therefore, is great if environmental policy is to have any real result in relieving the pressure on the environment. Unfortunately, however, many Member States lack the necessary administrative infrastructure capable of carrying out such monitoring.

This somewhat bleak picture of implementation and enforcement of environmental rules in the Community suggests that an alternative route is necessary. One suggestion is that as with competition law, the initiative should be given to individuals and companies. Undertakings should be encouraged to change their behaviour voluntarily in an environmentally friendly way, thereby reducing the need for administrative monitoring and enforcement.

The Commission's Fifth Environmental Action Programme, 'Towards Sustainability' takes provisional steps in this direction. Instead of stressing the 'top down approach' the Commission has cast the die towards what it calls the 'bottom up approach' emphasising companies' and individuals' responsibilities for their environment. The notion of 'shared responsibility' is stressed, which implies that undertakings should voluntarily act in an environmentally friendly way without being forced to do so by legislation. The Commission puts it like this:

'In facing up to the environmental challenges in this final decade of the millennium and in endeavouring to move towards a sustainable development path it is necessary to focus on the agents and activities which damage the environment and deplete the natural resource stock rather than wait, as has been the tendency in the past, for problems to emerge. As previously stated, this will require significant changes in current patterns of human consumption and behaviour. These objectives cannot be met by action at Community level alone, but rather on the basis of a sharing of responsibility at all levels of society including governments, regional and local authorities, non-governmental organisations, financial institutions, production, distribution and retail enterprises and individual citizens.'

The ways in which the behaviour of individuals and enterprises can be changed voluntarily are numerous. Education programmes, informational campaigns, tax incentives and advertising all have potential. Whilst giving full due to such methods, the Commission in its latest Action Programme focuses on enhancing the power of the market to fulfil its environmental policy. Not only can eco-industries be developed on the back of the 'environmentally friendliness' marketing handle, but also competition rules can be used both as a means of monitoring the environmental impact of firms' behaviour and agreements, and as a means of influencing those firms, products and processes which succeed and those which fail taking into account environmental criteria.

Environmental friendliness has already become an important marketing tool. By developing environmentally friendly products and integrating this aspect into existing goods and services, undertakings have increased their market overnight. Consumers have begun to take the environmental impact of a product or service into consideration. Once the polluter pays principle is enforced without discrimination, environmentally friendly products should also begin to have an edge on price.

Further, undertakings often have to deal with public authorities in the field of environmental protection. This may be through the application of specific standards of emissions from their plant, the treatment of waste or through the carrying out of prior environmental impact assessment. Undertakings may begin to cooperate so as to establish a common front when dealing with such public authorities. When such common front is for the benefit of the environment in environmental protection, a conflict may arise. The antipathy of competition law to cooperation between competitors may have to be balanced against the benefits of such cooperation to the environment.

Further, such a conflict may arise when competitors collaborate in the development of new environmentally friendly technology. This conflict takes on poignancy when it is remembered that a number of Community measures introduce the concept of 'best available technology not entailing excessive costs'. When competitors can argue that their collaboration has or will introduce new and better technology without excessive cost in pursuance of their environmental protection obligations, there may well be a strong argument that such benefits should provide a defence to violations of the competition rules arising out of the very collaboration itself.

The interaction of environmental law and competition policy has raised the possibility of the development of 'eco-industry'. Entrepreneurs have realised that environmentally friendly technologies are a new market with great potential. In its Fifth Environmental Action Programme, the Commission has written:

'The perceived conflict between environmental protection and economic competitiveness stems from a narrow view of the sources of prosperity and a static view of competition. Rather than reduce competitive advantage, stringent environmental requirements can actually enhance it by triggering upgrading and innovation.'

Further, in its Resolution concerning the relationship between industrial competitiveness and environmental protection, the Council acknowledges that policies to protect and improve the environment can stimulate the development and use of more efficient processes and can create markets for the new products and processes as well as adding to the costs of industry. The Council invited the Commission and Member States to cooperate to encourage the development of environmental technologies, including cleaner technologies and their diffusion to industry, including to smaller and medium sized enterprises in all regions of the Community. Investing in research activities to prevent pollution is, therefore, encouraged and may become very lucrative.

The purpose of this Part, therefore, is to investigate the various ways in which individuals and enterprises can take the initiative to protect the environment whilst maintaining the competitiveness of Community markets and industries. It should, however, be remembered that such individual action is not without its problems.

Not least, it is subject to the constraints of bureaucratic and judicial attitudes and to the judicial and administrative processes. As the Commission recognises in its latest action programme, just as the 'top down approach' has proved unsuccessful alone, so the 'bottom up approach' cannot exist without the backing of environmental legislation.

4.2 LEGAL BASES FOR THE LINK BETWEEN ENVIRONMENTAL PROTECTION AND COMPETITION LAW

The primary source of law in the EC is the EC Treaty as amended by the Treaty on European Union, which is of a framework nature. Power has been attributed to the Community by the Member States through the Treaty. This means that the Community can only act when it has authority to do so in one or more provisions of the Treaty. When empowered to do so, the Community authorities can legislate adding flesh onto the skeleton of the Treaty Provisions themselves. Although the types of measures which the Community authorities can legislate is not limited, the most common are those set out in Article 189EC - Regulations, Directives and Decisions.

In addition to the specific provisions in the Treaty, the European Court of Justice ('ECJ') (the judicial body of the Community) has ruled that implicit in the Treaty are a number of general principles which are derived from the legal systems of the Member States. These include, primarily, proportionality, necessity of action, fulfilment of legitimate expectations, and the general rules of natural justice.

The principal competition rules of the European Community are found in Articles 3(g), (l) and (n) and Articles 85-95EC inclusive. Article 3 sets out the general activities of the Community. Article 3(g) requires the Community to set up a system ensuring that competition in the internal market is not distorted. Articles 3(l) and (n) require the Community to strengthen the competitiveness of Community industry and to promote research and technological development respectfully. These activities are expanded upon in Articles 85-94. For present purposes, the principal Articles are 85 and 86. Article 85 prohibits agreements which restrict competition and have the potential of effecting trade between Member States. Such agreements may be exempted from this prohibition after investigation by the Commission. Article 86 prohibits undertakings with market power known as undertakings in a dominant position from abusing their power. Abuse includes both elimination of competitors and exploitation of customers and ultimate consumers.

Article 5 requires Member States to take all appropriate measures to ensure the fulfilment of the obligations arising out of the Treaty and obliges them to abstain from any measure which could jeopardise the attainment of the objectives of the Treaty. When this Article is combined with Article 3(g) and Articles 85 and 86, the result is that the Member States must not adopt or maintain measures which could deprive Articles 85 and 86 of their effectiveness. This has been reinforced by many judgments of the ECJ including Case 311/85, Vlaamse Reisbureaus [1987] ECR 3801.

Although no specific mention is made in the competition articles of the Treaty of the need to take environmental protection into account, this is implicit in the first sentence of Article 85(1). Instead of providing that restrictive agreements are incompatible with competition, it provides that such agreements 'shall be prohibited as incompatible with the Common Market' (emphasis added). Within the notion of 'the Common Market' are the objectives set out in Article 2 of the Treaty and the activities set out in Article 3 including Article 3(k), the Establishment of a Policy in the Sphere of the Environment.

Consequently, there is scope within the rules of competition law for the inclusion of environmental policy in competition decisions. Needless to say, there is scant evidence of this having been undertaken by the Commission in the past.

The rules relating to the protection of the environment in the Treaty are found in Articles 3(k) and Articles 130r-130t. For present purposes, the most significant provision is Article 130r(2):

'Environmental protection requirements must be integrated into the definition and implementation of other Community Policies.'

The original version of this provision prior to its amendment by the TEU, and as set out in the Single European Act provided that:

'Environmental protection requirements shall be a component of the Community's other policies.'

The amendment is not insignificant. In its original version, environmental policy was required to be no more than a consideration of competition policy. No indication is given as to at what stage environmental policy was to be taken into account or as to the relative wait to be given to environmental considerations. Although never tested before the ECJ, it would seem that provided that the Commission had taken into account the environmental considerations when taking decisions under Article 85 or 86, that would be sufficient. There was no obligation on the Commission to alter its decision based on competition grounds should the environmental consequences offer an alternative decision. By substituting the original version by 'environmental protection requirements must be integrated into the definition and implementation of other Community policies' mere consideration without action will no longer be sufficient. In short DGIV (the division of the Commission responsible for competition policy) must redefine its competition policy so as to satisfy the objective of environmental protection. Further, its competition decisions must be consistent with the requirements of environmental protection. In short, it is no longer sufficient for the Commission to take its decision solely on the basis of the effects on the competitiveness of the market of a given agreement. Needless to say, this provision has not yet been litigated before the ECJ. Much of what follows, therefore, is somewhat speculative but it is intended to suggest a number of approaches which might be taken on the basis of these Articles.

By way of background, a brief description of both the Community's environmental policy and of its competition policy follows. The Chapter then goes on to investigate ways in which the application of Articles 85, 86, 90, 92 and 130r-t may be altered to satisfy the new requirements arising out of the link between competition policy and environmental protection.

4.3 ENVIRONMENTAL POLICY WITHIN THE EC

There are four principal institutions of the Community. The fifth institution is the Court of Auditors which is of little relevance for present purposes. The Council of Ministers is the intergovernmental body of the Community. It is the primary legislator although there is no close analogy with the UK Parliament in that the Members are not directly or democratically elected. Indeed, the Council of

Ministers is true to its name and consists of the Heads of Government or State and Governmental Ministers of the Member States. Although it is the primary legislator, the Council of Ministers does not have the right to propose and therefore to initiate the legislation.

The Commission is the supranational institution of the EC. Although its officials are drawn from the Member States, they are required to relinquish their national prejudices and to become 'European'. The Commission is the bureaucracy of the Community. In addition it has the sole right to initiate legislation, it is required to supervise the enforcement of EC law (Article 155 EC), it can in some cases take quasi-judicial decisions and also pass delegated legislation.

The European Parliament is perhaps the weakest of the four principal institutions. Originally not directly elected, its members have largely an advisory function. The democratic deficit in the method of election has largely been resolved with the institution of direct elections and now finds expression in the very minor legislative role accorded to the EP. Recent changes in the legislative procedures available to the EC system through the Single European Act (SEA) 1986 and the Treaty on European Union (TEU) 1993, have addressed this problem only in part.

The fourth principal EC Institution is the Court of Justice (ECJ) which sits in Luxembourg. It is the main judicial body of the EC with an administrative as well as a judicial function. Since 1989 it has been divided into two, with the Court of First Instance (CFI) hearing competition law and staff cases, and the full ECJ with jurisdiction to hear all other applications.

Turning to environmental policy, the founding Treaty of Rome in 1957 made no mention of the environment. The omission was perhaps a consequence of the time. The idea of environmental protection as understood today did not exist. Certainly there is no necessary contradiction between the management of Europe's economy and its markets on the one hand, and the environment on the other. Only two Articles can be interpreted as offering some kind of link to environmental policy. The first was Article 2 which set as one of the Community's objectives the 'harmonious development of economic activities and a balanced expansion'. In a general way, therefore, a reference is made to a desire to maintain and improve the quality of life of the citizens of Europe. Article 36 is more specific but also more negative. It provides for the continuation or introduction of restrictions on the movement of trade within the EC for reasons of public health and the protection of animals and plants. The reference is clearly limited giving the breadth of 'the environment'.

Neither of these provisions could be treated as a legal basis for secondary legislation. All was not lost, however, and with a little imagination and ingenuity, two other Articles were adopted by the Commission as the grounds for proposing environmentally oriented measures: Articles 100 and 235. Article 100 empowered the Council on a proposal from the Commission and having consulted the Parliament to issue Directives for the approximation of laws, regulations or administrative provisions of the Member States to remove barriers to trade and distortions of competition. Article 235 empowers the Council to take appropriate action to attain one of the objectives of the EC when the Treaty itself is silent.

It was therefore as a result of the need to ensure a level competitive playing field in the European markets that environmental legislation first came onto the EC statute books. The first piece of legislation came in 1967 with a Directive on the classification, packaging and labelling of dangerous substances (Council Directive 67/548, OJ [1967] L196).

Such an approach was limited, however, by the need to find an economic peg on which to hang the environmental measure. In essence, environmental policy was parasitic to the harmonisation objective. There had to be some trade or market based reason for the measure. A purely environmental concern was not sufficient.

The first explicit environmental breakthrough came in 1972 at a summit of the Community Heads of State and Government in Paris. The Ministers stressed the reference in Article 2 EEC that economic expansion should equally result in an improvement in the quality of life and that to this end particular attention should be given to environmental protection. They proposed that the Commission should draw up an action plan in 1973 in tandem with programmes for social and regional policy and consumer protection. So it was that Community environmental policy was born.

At the time of writing, we have entered the Fifth Environmental Action Programme and have seen two significant amendments to the EC Treaty specifically working environmental policy and environmental protection into the objectives of the Community.

4.3.2 THE ACTION PROGRAMMES

The Action Programmes represent the basic charter for Community and Environmental Policy. Each Action Programme covers a period of four to five years. They are proposed by the Commission and adopted by the Council of Ministers in the form of a 'resolution'. They are not legally binding. Instead, they set out the agenda for Community legislative action to be taken under the specific legal basis provided in the EC Treaty. The action programmes are published in the 'C' series of the Official Journal.

The First Action Programme was adopted on the 22nd November 1973 and covered the years 1973 to 1976 (OJ [1973] C112). It defined for the first time the basic principles and objectives of Community Environmental Policy, and is therefore often viewed as the most important programme. The changes made by the Fifth Action Programme are, however, equally important.

In its introduction, the First Action Programme affirms the objectives set out in the preamble to and in Article 2 of the Treaty of Rome including 'the constant improvement of the living and working conditions of peoples [of the Member States]', and 'the harmonious development of their economies'. The objectives were specified as including the prevention, reduction and, as far as possible, elimination of pollution and nuisances; avoidance of damage to the ecological balance by exploitation of resources; and seeking common solutions to environmental problems with States outside the Community.

A number of basic principles were also established. These included the preventive and precautionary principle; the polluter pays principle; respect for the interests of third countries including the developing world; environmental education; and an oblique reference to sustainable development.

Three categories of action were singled out by the Commission within the framework of Community Environmental Policy. These were action to reduce and prevent pollution and nuisances; action to improve the quality of the environment; and action in international organisations.

The Second Action Programme was adopted on 17th May 1977 and covered the years 1977-1981 (OJ [1977] C139). In essence the Programme was a continuation and expansion of the objectives and actions taken under the First Programme reaffirming the latter's general principles and objectives.

The Third Environmental Action Programme for the years 1982-1986 was adopted on the 7th February 1983 (OJ [1983] C46). The Programme built on the previous two, introducing four new elements. The first was the integration of environmental policy into other sectoral policies of the Community such as transport, energy, research etc. The Programme emphasised, therefore, the economic and social aspects of environmental policy, particularly the fact that it should contribute to lessening current economic problems such as employment. The second new element was an explicit introduction of prior environmental impact assessment of projects. The third new characteristic was the singling-out of several priority areas including the integration of the environmental dimension into other Community policies, encouraging the development of clean technology, and policy on waste disposal. The fourth aspect of the Third Action Programme involved the listing of certain considerations which the Commission should use as a basis for drawing up proposals. These considerations included recognition of the different economic and ecological conditions and structures existing in the Community's regions.

The Fourth Action Programme began in 1987 and ran until the end of 1992. It assumed a new format highlighting the different conceptual approaches in the area of pollution control and prevention, including the multi-media approach, the substance directed approach, the pollution source directed approach etc. It also embodied new content developing a number of new principles and ideas. An example is the development of new environmental standards which are sufficiently strict to have a lasting effect on the quality of the environment. Such standards were seen as effective only when they had become an economic necessity for Community industry and were therefore interwoven into the market. A second new aspect found in the Fourth Action Programme was the need to give greater importance to the control and practical implementation of Community Directives affecting the environment. Environmental education and information were also given new impetus.

The Fourth Action Programme built on the Third, in particular by emphasising the need to integrate environmental protection into the other Community policies, specifically mentioning employment, agriculture, transport and development.

The current Fifth Action Programme runs from 1993 to 1997 (OJ [1993] C138). In many ways the latest Action Programme is as important as the first. In particular it marks a significant shift in emphasis away from the legislative top down approach to an integrated bottom up approach involving all other policy sectors and all levels of action. The Commission's terminology reflects that used when referring to subsidiarity and the analogy is no accident. To quote from the Fifth Action Programme: 'Towards sustainability':

'This Programme itself constitutes a turning point for the Community. Just as the challenge of the 1980's was completion of the internal market, the reconciliation of the environment and development is one of the principal challenges facing the Community in the World at large in the 1990's. 'Towards sustainability' is not a programme for the Commission alone, nor one geared towards the environmentalists alone. It provides a framework for a new approach to the environment and to economic and social activity and development, and requires positive will at all levels of the political and corporate spectrums and the involvement of all members of the public active as citizens and consumers in order to make it work'. (paragraph 39).

The idea is that, through better education and dissemination of information about the environment, each and every one of us should have a greater say in deciding how the environment should be treated. This may come about through activity in environmentally oriented NGO's, using our rights as citizens of the Community to lobby M.P's and M.E.P's and Members of the Commission and also when making decisions as consumers. Products in the shops should carry more information about their effects on the environment both during manufacture, use and at the point of disposal. Consumers should have more opportunities to dispose of waste in environmentally friendly ways and should have the chance to discriminate between products on the basis of their manufacturer's environmental strategies. The list of opportunities should, reading between the lines of 'Towards Sustainability', be endless.

At the corporate level, the Commission envisages greater economic pressures on market participants arising out of the environmental dimension. This may be through higher environmental standards for products; prior environmental impact assessment; environmental auditing and quality assurances similar to the UK Management Quality Assurance BS5750; environmental taxes and subsidies on energy and natural resources geared to the environmental consequences; site and plant location decisions; waste disposal and recycling obligations; and liability regimes designed to make the polluter pay. Each one of these pressures will have the effects on the relevant markets and eventually all markets in the Community. So it is, that the competition strategy and policy of firms will be affected.

Whilst the Fifth Programme instigates a change in emphasis in environmental policy, the classical approach outlined in the four earlier programmes has not been abandoned altogether. 'Towards Sustainability' includes a comprehensive legislative strategy with complex timetabling leading up to the end of the century. Like the Fourth Programme, it adopts priority areas, some old like energy, transport, agriculture, waste and water, and some new, like tourism. Certainly, the principles developed during the first 20 years of active Community Environmental Policy continued to provide the foundations for the EC Strategies. The polluter pays, the precautionary principle and the rectification of pollution and damage at source principle reverberate throughout the 1993 documents.

It is therefore an overstatement to say that the approach of the Fifth Action Programme is brand new. For example, the integration of policies has always been an element in the Community approach to environmental protection, if not the hallmark. It is the emphasis that has changed. One writer has felt it appropriate to say that the Community no longer has an 'environmental' policy but a policy of 'sustainability' or more accurately sustainable development and growth. Such is the general impression left by the Fifth Action Programme.

4.3.2 THE IMPORTANCE OF ENVIRONMENTAL POLICY IN THE EC

The status of environmental policy within the Community is as yet unresolved. In a number of cases and in Article F of the TEU the

ECJ and the Community have accepted the need to respect the fundamental human rights as embodied in the European Convention on Human Rights and in the common constitutional traditions of the Member States when applying and implementing the Community's policies. In this sense the fundamental human rights form part of the constitutional law of the EC. Community rules must defer to these rights should a conflict arise. The unresolved question is whether the Community's environmental policy has assumed a similar constitutional character to fundamental human rights within the EC order or whether it is to be treated as one of the other major policies for community such as the social policy, agricultural policy and competition policy.

The ECJ has not yet been asked to consider this question. The drafting of the Treaty Articles devoted to environmental policy is, however, unique. Most significantly, Article 130r(2) is the only Article which requires express integration of one policy, namely, the environmental policy, into both the definition and implementation of all other policies. Such wording appears to have the character of a constitution.

On the other hand, to place the protection of the environment on the same level as constitutional principles such as subsidiarity and fundamental human rights would be a bold move. For example, the European Convention of Human Rights does not recognise a fundamental right to a clean environment.

This issue is not one of academic interest only. It will be of crucial importance when conflicts between the requirements of competition policy and those of environmental protection arise. Some means of prioritising between the two sets of rules is necessary. If environmental policy has a constitutional function and status then in such a conflict it should prevail if, as is argued below, competition policy does not enjoy such a constitutional status. The cases which have come before the ECJ in which such a conflict has existed have either been decided in favour of the environmental interest or the Court has found that the environmental measures claimed have been disproportionate or discriminatory on national grounds and therefore offensive for a reason different from that being discussed at present. In essence, the Court avoided the question.

An example is the Danish beer bottle case, Case 302/86 Commission v Denmark [1988] ECR 4607. Article 30EC prohibits quantitative restrictions on the importation of goods. The Court has held that some exceptions have to be recognised to this prohibition in the present state of the law where the rules of the Member States have not been harmonized. Examples have included consumer protection or to prevent fiscal fraud. In addition, Article 36 of the Treaty excludes from the ambit of Article 30 restrictions adopted in order to protect human health and the life of animals. In the Danish beer bottle case, the Commission argued that a Danish law requiring beer to be sold in containers of a particular shape and to be returnable was a breach of Article 30 of the Treaty. The Danish Government counter-argued that the system adopted which was not an absolute system, was set up for the protection of the environment. The ECJ recognised that environmental considerations had to be taken into account. It accepted that protection of the environment was 'a mandatory requirement' which may limit the application of Article 30. The ECJ accepted that the restriction on the type of bottles to be used, and the recycling obligations in order to protect the countryside and to preserve materials were justified in the interests of protecting the environment. The rules set up a composite system which is necessary to achieve the legitimate aim. Those rules were not regarded as being disproportionate save the limitation on the number of bottles which could be imported other than those of the permitted type was held to be too restrictive. The requirements of environmental protection triumphed over the principle of free movement of goods.

In the Walloon Waste Import Ban case, Case C-2/90, Commission v Belgium, the Court was asked to declare that rules adopted by Belgium for the disposal of waste were contrary to Community law. The Court held that all waste, whether recyclable or not, had to be treated as a product the free movement of which could not in principle be restricted pursuant to Article 30. It accepted on the other hand, that the accumulation of waste could be a danger to the environment so that the mandatory requirement of environmental protection was well founded. The Court rejected the Commission's contention that the mandatory requirements were applied in a discriminatory way. It ruled that the principle that environmental damage should as a priority be rectified at source, as established by Article 130r(2) of the Treaty implied that it was up to each region, commune or other local authority to take the measures appropriate to ensure the reception, treatment and disposal of its own waste. Such waste therefore had to be disposed of as close as possible to the place of its production in order to limit its transport to a minimum. In view of the differences between waste produced in one place and that produced in another the Court held that the disputed measures could not be regarded as discriminatory. In essence, waste from one place is different from waste of another place.

In another case the German authorities had undertaken work to protect the coastline and to alter dykes. A result of their doing so, it was alleged, had affected the protection of wild birds contrary to the provisions of various Community directives. The Court found that the Commission had known about the proposed works since 1984. The works had begun in 1986. It was only in 1989 when two-thirds of the work had been done that the Commission brought proceedings before the Court. By the time an application was made for an Injunction there remained little work to be done and the Court refused the interim application substantially on that ground. In the final determination, the Court again accepted that the works were limited to the minimum and that there had been a very small reduction of the land reserved to protect wild birds. It was accepted that the protection of human life would justify an interference with the habitat of wild birds, but to interfere merely to provide improved access for fishing boats was in principle incompatible with the provisions of the Directive and environmental policy. In the end the Court found that there had been compensatory steps taken in fact so that overall, the damage to the habitat protected for wild birds was not substantially changed. Although this case appears to be one in which the requirements of environmental protection lost, the case turned on its particular facts. Arguably, had the application for interim measures been made much earlier, the Court may have taken a very different decision.

In another German case, however, environmental interests did not prevail. The German authorities imposed a road tax on vehicles using the motorways in such a way as to discriminate against vehicles from Member States other than Germany. Germany relied upon the justification that the monies were required in order to improve the environment. The Court rejected this argument. It was plainly discriminatory legislation. The risk of businesses outside Germany going into liquidation or suffering substantial financial loss was a serious one on the facts. The measure taken was disproportionate and discriminatory. It was on these grounds that the environmental argument was rejected. Notably, the Court decided that environmental protection could have been achieved by other means.

These cases indicate one of two things. Either that at the present stage in the development of EC law, environmental protection as a policy of the EC does not rank alongside the traditional economic policies which have been the foundation of the EC's first thirty-five years existence, or that the Court has not yet been seised of an appropriate case in which to grasp the nettle in the priority debate. The only conclusion to be reached at present, therefore, is that the issue is unclear. This topic is given a second airing in Part 4.6 below.

4.4 COMPETITION POLICY WITHIN THE EC

The basic expression of Community competition policy in the EC Treaty is in Article 3(g): 'the activities of the Community shall include a system ensuring that competition in the internal market is not distorted.' The introduction to the ninth Report on Competition Policy, although published 14 years ago, remains an authoritative statement of Commission policy on competition. It stated that the first fundamental objective of competition policy is to keep the Common Market open and unified. In the early stages, the need to integrate the national product markets of the Member States had a profound effect upon the content of EC Competition policy. In particular, the need to integrate often eclipsed economic analysis in the Commission's implementation of Articles 85 and 86EC.

The second fundamental objective identified by the Commission was the need to maintain 'the right amount of competition in order for the Treaty's requirements to be met and its aims attained'. This suggests an interventionist approach and advances the argument that markets are incapable of maintaining a competitive structure alone. In particular, the Commission is concerned that it conserve market opportunities for small and medium sized enterprises. In addition, the Commission looks to the fairness in the market place, especially with regard to State subsidies under Article 92EC, and the need to protect the interests of workers, users and consumers.

Consequently, the Commission's aim is not to achieve perfect competition. Rather, the aim is 'workable competition' in which a degree of concentration in any given market is carefully monitored to prevent monopoly or oligopoly, whilst not requiring markets to be atomistic.

The same question as posed to the status of environmental policy can be raised in the context of competition policy. In essence, is competition policy merely a tool for the achievement of other ends, or is it part of the constitutional law of the Community?

Again, it is necessary to consider the ECJ's approach to the position of economic rights as constitutional principles of the EC. In a number of cases undertakings or individuals have claimed rights, such as those guaranteed by national constitutions in the European Convention on the Protection of Human Rights, including a right to property, the freedom to pursue a trade or professional activity, and have argued that such rights are protected from intervention in the market by the Commission.

In case 44/79, Hauer v Land Rhineland-Phalz [1980] 3 CMLR 42, a wine grower argued that a Council Regulation prohibiting the planting of new vines in certain areas infringed her right to property and was therefore unlawful. This prohibition meant that market entry and expansion were restricted. In essence, expansion was only possible through the purchase of existing production facilities rather than through the creation of new vineyards. The Court's approach was modelled on the policy in Protocol No.1 of the European Convention on Human Rights. The Court recognised a limit on the right to private property dictated by the needs of the general interest. The intervention on the market did not, therefore, deprive Mrs. Hauer of a right to property since the property could be used in other lawful ways. Further, justification for the limitation to the right was found to be in the 'general interests'. A similar justification could be found in national legislation relating to agriculture and forestry laws, and to water, environmental and planning legislation.

It could be seen, therefore, that the limitations arising from the application of competition policy could be justified on similar grounds. In the Hauer case, the Advocate General examined the 'economic sacrifice' demanded of the individuals affected by the authorities' intervention. He found that:

'It is a matter of common experience that agricultural land is mostly capable of being put to various uses, even though not all such uses offer the same degree of profitability ... The fact that the Community prohibitions precluded a more advantageous use is unimportant, since in order to show that the Community measure was not in the nature of an expropriation it is sufficient that in spite of that measure the land retained an appreciable economic value'. (Para 8 of the AG's Opinion).

This same approach could be taken to any tradable asset, not just agricultural land. There is, therefore, on this basis a strong argument that competition policy is not limited by the right to property and may be developed and applied so as to reduce the value or limit the range of uses of property unless, in an individual case, the intervention amounts to a complete expropriation.

A similar approach is found in cases under Article 215EC for compensation for damages arising out of actions impairing the value of trading assets. The Court has refused to entertain such claims, holding that the substance of the rights of property has not been infringed, and that the detrimental effect to the property was 'merely an indirect consequence of a policy with which the aims of the general public interests are pursued which vary greatly depending upon the economic factors effecting market trends'. (See Case 59/83 Biovilac SA v Commission [1977] 2 CMLR 881). Similarly, the Court has stated in Case 83/76 Bayerische HNL Vermehrungsbetriebe v Commission & Council [1978] 3 CMLR 565:

'Individuals may be required, in the sectors coming within the Economic Policy of the Community, to accept within reasonable limits certain harmful effects on their economic interests as a result of a legislative measure without being able to obtain compensation from public funds'.

Restrictions on the right to pursue a trade have been examined in Case 230/78, Eridania v Minister of Agriculture [1979] ECR 2749. Once again, the Court accepted that this right may be limited by the requirements of the 'general interests'. However, the Court drew a very strong distinction between the right to participate in a market and the right to any guaranteed level of economic rents. In Case 4/73 Nold v Commission [1974] 2 CMLR 338, the Court stated:

'As concerns the guarantees given to individuals ..., they could in no case be extended to the protection of mere commercial interests or prospects, the contingent character of which is inherent in the very essence of economic activity'.

Through examination of such cases, it appears therefore, that competition policy is not limited by Community constitutional norms. On the other hand, however, neither does it appear that competition law is or can be described as constitutional. It is not used as a means of creating and maintaining a certain form of preferred economic system. Competition policy in the Community is only one method of achieving the overall aim set down in Article 2EC. Other policies, including industrial, agricultural and social policies, seek to achieve similar goals through different methods. In addition, the acceptance of a strongly regulatory regime for the agricultural sector prevents the free market notion being characterised as a community constitutional norm. Furthermore, in the market for labour, although the Community system provides for the free movement of resources, it does not provide for a system of production related remuneration. The converse is true. The Social Charter requires that 'all employment shall be fairly remunerated ... A decent wage shall be established' (emphasis added).

4.5ENVIRONMENTAL LAW AND WORKABLE COMPETITION.

The importance of an active environmental policy to the achievment of the objectives of competition law, and in particular the establishment of a level playing field in competition within the Common Market, can be seen in the very origins of EC Environmental law. In the absence of specific provisions dealing with the environment in the 1957 Treaty of Rome, the Commission within a decade of its inception saw the need to harmonise rules concerning the protection of the environment so as to avoid distortions of competition. If in one territory an undertaking is able to produce goods without internalising the environmental costs it will have a competitive advantage over manufacturers in different territories which are obliged to pay for environmental clean up and proper waste disposal. In short, without taking into account the environmental costs, goods will be falsely priced leading to an inefficient allocation of resources and distortions of the normal market mechanism.

It is important, therefore that not only are the rules on environmental protection harmonised throughout the Community, but that they are applied consistently and without discrimination. This is, however, where the Community's approach comes unstuck.

In the first 20 years of Community environmental policy, more than 200 legislative measures have been issued in the field of environmental protection, the majority of such being in the form of directives. By Article 189 EC, directives require national implementation to become effective. Member States have, however, proved reluctant to implement the majority of these directives correctly or within the time period laid down. Thus distortions in the competitive playing field are created.

If a Member State does not implement a directive by the deadline specified in the measure, the Commission can initiate proceedings before the Court under Article 169. This procedure is both slow and cumbersome. Lord Slynn (Judge of the ECJ) has suggested that some form of judgment in default of defence or by consent to avoid the normal processes of litigation should be introduced. The slow process of full pleadings, hearing, and an Advocate General's opinion, could be short-circuited.

Many cases have been brought under the Article 169 procedure, including provisions relating to the quality of bathing waters, the control of exhaust fumes, and the disposal of waste. A point of interest is that every Member State has been brought before the Court under Article 169 for failure to implement an environmental directive. In many such cases there is no real defence. In circumstances where nothing has been done to implement the directive the Court's task is easy, but becomes more difficult where the Member State has made some attempt to comply with its obligations. Two questions then arise. Firstly, the nature of the obligation on the Member State, and secondly, whether, there is evidence that the Member State has not sufficiently complied with the obligation as so defined.

Nevertheless, the Court has been vigorous in its judgments. It has consistently refused to accept administrative, political and institutional difficulties as an excuse for non-performance. In Case 380/87 Enichem v Cinisello Balsamo [1989] ECR 2491, the Mayor of a commune had forbidden the use of plastic bags which were not biodegradable except for the disposal of waste. Traders sought to quash the edict. The question raised was whether it was necessary for the State to notify the Commission of all regulations made or to notify only those of practical and extensive importance. It was argued that a matter of such limited effect could not have been intended to be covered by the relevant directive and that it was not possible for decentralised authorities like communes to give such notice to the

Commission. The Court found that the Directive in question contained no exemptions or derogations and that the Directive must therefore apply to all institutions of the State, even to decentralised ones like the Mayor of a commune.

One criticism that has previously been levelled at the Article 169 proceedings has been rectified by the TEU. Until the amendments in 1993, there was no sanction for a State's failure to implement directives. The new Article 171 EC now provides for the Court to fine a Member State found to be in breach of its obligations in Article 169 proceedings. The effectiveness of this new power has not yet been tested.

Further, Member States have the possibility of bringing similar actions before the Court against each other under Article 170 EC. These however are rare indeed, most probably on account of the political sensitivity involved.

The major criticism laid against Article 169 proceedings is the time delay. The proceedings in the East London River Crossing case and the dispute over Twyford Down in Winchester show how long these proceedings can take. Often protracted negotiations take place as Member States seek to settle instead of going before the Court.

In short, therefore, the adoption of a measure to protect the environment is by no means a guarantee that the measure will be applicable in the Member States and that therefore distortions of competition will have been ironed out. Indeed, the converse is probably true.

When a directive is finally implemented into national law problems continue to arise. The enforcement of environmental legislation by its very nature is often difficult. The first major obstacle is that of cost. Frequently those concerned with bringing actions do not have the resources to follow up violations of the relevant environmental legislation. Secondly, the burden of enforcement frequently lies with public authorities, because environmental legislation is by its nature general and rarely does it confer rights on individuals. Often national authorities have neither the personnel nor the mechanisms to properly and effectively monitor compliance with environmental legislation.

In conclusion, therefore, as for the need to have environmental legislation to assist in the creation of a level playing field for competition, the problems of implementation and enforcement mean that any new measure can create as many problems as it solves. Only when there is an effective method of ensuring compliance by Member States and individuals with the ever increasing portfolio of environmental legislation, will the distortions of competition be ironed out.

Environmental policy has created another dimension relevant to competition law. This is the establishment of what is known as 'eco-industry'. The Commission in its Fifth Action Programme has described the situation as follows:

'Depending on their nature, virtually all enterprises use natural resources for their processes and products, create various types and qualities of waste, and contribute to the pollution of air, water and soil. In limited cases only have the long-term costs of these resources of the pollution so far been internalized in the costs of operating the plant or in the price of the final product or service. It is clear that the perpetuation of the situation is not viable on either economic or environmental grounds. There is a growing awareness that industry's own interest is at stake; increasing demand for clean technologies and products will create new market opportunities, with particular advantages for innovational industries; industry also sees the advantages in terms of savings on resources and energy, where environmental considerations are integrated into management policy.'

In recent years a new industry has been developed - the 'eco-industry'. In essence this 'eco industry' comprises new technologies designed to protect the environment or to render special environmental services.

The products and services of this new industry will compete with those of existing industries. Financially, however, and this is the Commission's hope, demand for the products of these clean technologies will overtake that for the products and services of existing industries as the polluter pays principle is fully implemented and environmental awareness grows among the populace. It would seem, therefore, important that the rules of competition law are applied to ensure that the price mechanism in markets operates properly and that the older established industries do not behave in such a way as to hinder the market entry and development of this new eco industry.

In conclusion the Council's Resolution concerning the relationship between industrial competitiveness and environmental protection (OJ [1992] C331/5) invites the Commission and Member States to:

(a) Cooperate to encourage the development of environmental technologies, including cleaner technologies and their diffusion to industry, including to smaller medium sized enterprises in all regions of the Community;

(b) Give greater emphasis to the development of environmental technologies including cleaner technologies within existing or plant programmes for the support of research and development relevant to industrial processes.

4.6 COMPETITION LAW AND ENVIRONMENTAL PROTECTION

The first point to be made is that there is no basis in Community law for exempting measures which are aimed at environmental protection from the rules of competition law.

Although a growing 'eco-industry' is discernable, this has no specific basis in the EC Treaty. Even if an argument could be made that a new sector of activity on a par with coal and steel, military industries, agriculture and transport, has been fashioned out of the past 20 years of Community environmental policy there is no provision in the Treaty exempting it from the rules of competition law. Those sectors which are so excluded are given a privileged position in a specific Treaty Article. For example 232(1) EC excludes the coal and steel sector, Article 223(1)(b) excludes military industries, Article 42 excludes agriculture and Articles 74 and 84 EC excludes to a certain extent transport from the rules of competition. The Council has power to disapply this exclusion. Nevertheless, eco industries do not fall into the same category. Like any other sector, the competition rules apply.

Since, however, the application of competition rules to a given sector is intended to lead to a situation where resources are allocated in the most efficient way, this should benefit eco-industries. The aim of the eco-industry is to develop products which are environmentally friendly. This should distinguish such products from those produced by the classical old industries. The application of the polluter pays principle should result in prices which reflect the environmental consequences of any given product. Eventually there should come a time when the high quality products of the eco-industry are cheaper than those of competing older industries. In this sense, therefore, competition law can be seen as an efficient instrument for the protection of the environment.

As has been discussed above, a system created by the amendments to the Treaty of Rome by the Single European Act 1986 and later the Treaty on European Union 1993, requires the integration of the requirements of environmental protection into the definition and implementation of competition policy. Furthermore, when taking decisions under Articles 85 and 86, the Commission is obliged to consider the objectives of the Common Market and not just a purist's understanding of competition law. This means that the Commission cannot restrict itself to an economic and market based analysis when taking competition law decisions.

This of course raises the question referred to above of how it is that the Commission will resolve conflicts between the requirements of environmental protection and its own brand of competition policy in any given case. The Court has given no definitive guidance as to the priority to be given to the requirements of environmental protection and those of competition policy respectfully. A suggestion made above is that competition law is not a constitutional norm and is therefore subject to the requirements of more fundamental obligations imposed upon the Community. Further, it has been argued that environmental protection is one of those fundamental rights. Clearly, it is recognised that such an approach is both progressive and lacking in authority.

In the area of human rights, the ECJ has had to deal with conflicts between the economic rights protected by the Treaty, such as the free movement of goods, the free movement of persons and the right of establishment on the one hand, and the fundamental human rights protected by national constitutional law and/or the European Convention on Human Rights, on the other. Examples include Case 5/88, Wachauf [1989] ECR 2609, in which the Court had to deal with the question of whether it would be contrary to the fundamental rights principal protecting private property for a lessee to be deprived without compensation of his right to payment for stopping milk production under EC Regulations; Case 159/90, Society for the

Protection of the Unborn Child (Ireland) Limited v Grogan et al. [1991] 3 CMLR 849 in which the Court was asked whether national associations can be prohibited from informing its citizens about the possibility for abortions abroad or whether such a prohibition was an illegitimate restriction on the freedom to provide services as defined in Article 59 EC Treaty. The prohibition of abortion was a direct consequence of the right to life as it was formulated in the Irish Constitution. Similarly in C-260/89, Greek Television Elliniki Radiophonia Tileorassi v Dimotiki Etairia Pliroforissis [1992] ECR I-2925, the question for the Court was whether certain exclusive rights to transmit television programmes in Greece were compatible with the freedom to supply services.

In these cases, along with numerous other examples, the approach of the Court has been to acknowledge the existence of fundamental human rights within the Member States' constitutions, and to give expression to that recognition by allowing limited derogations from the economic principles protected by the Treaty. The Court's approach has been modelled on that of the European Convention of Human Rights. In the Convention, fundamental human rights are protected subject to restricted exceptions which must, in general, be prescribed by law, pursue a legitimate aim and be necessary in a democratic society.

So in the Wachauf case, the Court repeated that fundamental rights principles were part of Community law, but that some limited restrictions may be imposed on those rights. The Court found, however, that the lessee's loss of his rights was not due to the Community rules themselves but to the way in which the German Government had implemented them. In the Grogan case, the Court avoided the need to decide between competing rules by finding that the services offered by Mr Grogan and his student friends fell outside the scope of the EC Treaty. Those services had been provided for free and therefore lacked the necessary economic content to cross the threshold of EC law. In the Greek Television case, the Court pointed out that freedom to supply services was subject to exceptions on grounds of public policy, public security and public health, under Article 56 EC. It went on to hold that where a right is given by Community law and is subject to exceptions for specific purposes such as the freedom to provide services, national legislation setting out those exceptions must comply with Community fundamental rights principles.

Although in cases dealing with fundamental rights the Court has had to deal with conflicts between competing rights, the judgments can be distinguished from the present case. The distinction lies in the source of the competing rights. Although the Court has held that fundamental human rights form part of the Community legal order, they do not stem explicitly from the Treaty. Their source is in the constitutional foundations of the Member States and international treaties such as the European Convention on Human Rights. Where the obligations to protect the environment and to ensure competition within the Common Market is not distorted are concerned, both rights and obligations arise out of the Treaty itself. The question is not one of prioritising between what are in essence national rights and Community rights but between two Community rights. The 'derogation solution' found to be convenient in the area of human rights is not so readily available.

Employment rights provides another example in which conflicts between Community policies have arisen. In particular, as the Community Social Charter states, one aim of this area of Community policy is that 'all employment shall be <u>fairly</u> remunerated ... a <u>decent</u> wage shall be established' (emphasis added) (Article 8, Community Charter of Fundamental Social Rights). The concepts of fairness and decency are not necessarily linked to the economic value of labour. In essence, in the market for jobs, market forces are not given free reign. Further, the Community's legislative code in the area of social policy directly embodies, and is sustained by, the principle of equality. In Case 248/83, <u>Commission v Germany</u> [1985] ECR 1459, the Court stated at ground 16:

'Like Article 119 of the EEC Treaty, Directives [75/117] (Equal Pay) and [76/207] (Equal Treatment) are of general application, a fact which is inherent in the very nature of the principle which they laid down. New cases of discrimination may not be created by exempting certain groups of the provisions intended to guarantee equal treatment for men and women in working life as a whole'.

Those directives, together with the Court's case, mean that in the market for labour, a fundamental principle of quality is applied not only to national administrations but to each and every employer. The Community's brand of equality has particular characteristics which mean that the restrictions on normal market forces operating in the labour market go both deep and wide. For example, differences inherent in the sexes cannot be used as grounds for discrimination.

In Case 177/88 Dekker v VJV-Centrum [1990] ECR 3841 and Case 179/88 Hartz v Aldi [1990] ECR 3879, the Court ruled that pregnancy discrimination constituted direct sex discrimination. A woman could not be dismissed purely on the grounds of pregnancy even though a man incapacitated for a similar period of time could lose his job. Men cannot be pregnant, therefore to treat a woman differently from a man because she can be pregnant is direct discrimination.

Similarities between the sexes must also be protected. This means that there is a presumption that men and women are the same. Should a woman be treated differently from man in a similar situation, the burden lies on the employer to show that the circumstances of the man and that of the woman were different, justifying the apparent discrimination - see Article 2(2) of Directive 76/207. Where grounds for derogation from the principle of equality are proven, the Court will require that the steps taken are shown to have been necessary in a specific case and to have conformed to the principle of proportionality. So in Case 222/84, Johnston v RUC [1986] ECR 1651, the UK Government argued that it was justified in allowing a blanket exclusion of women from employment as Police in the Royal Ulster Constabulary on grounds such as the need to protect women from violence and the fact that they may be used as hostages in a sensitive political context of Northern Ireland. The Court rejected the UK's claim to a general derogation on the grounds of public safety. The Court held that public safety may justify derogation under Article 2(2) of the Equal Treatment Directive (76/207) provided that:

'The derogation remain within the limits of what is appropriate and necessary for achieving the aim in view and [that] ... the principle of equal treatment be reconciled as far as possible with the requirements of that [aim]'.

In the area of social policy, the Community has drastically restricted competition in the market for labour. It has done so on the basis that men and women should be treated equally and that the objections set out in Article 2 EC, that a high standard of living should be attained for Community citizens, must be protected. Such objectives conflict with the notion of free competition. The latter has therefore been sidelined in favour of the former.

To draw an analogy between the integration of environmental policy into competition law on the one hand and the Community's social policy on the other may be like walking on quick sand. First, at its inception, the Community's social policy was treated as an objective equal to the economic aspect of the Community's raison d'etre. In the seminal case of the Community's social policy, Case 43/76 Defrenne v Sabena [1976] ECR 454, the Court interpreted Article 119 EC, which requires equality between the sexes and pay, as embodying a double aim, with the consequences that:

'This double aim, which is at once economic and social, shows that the principle of equal pay forms part of the foundations of the Community.'

In the second Defrenne case, (Case 149/177), Defrenne v Sabena (2) [1978] ECR 1365, the Court expanded the principle of equal pay into a general fundamental right of equality. It declared that 'respect for fundamental personal human rights is one of the general principles of Community law ... There can be no doubt that the elimination of discrimination based on sex forms part of those fundamental rights.' The pedigree of the labour market in the Community, therefore, is different from the markets in goods and services. In the latter the approach has been one of free competition subject to some limited policy restrictions in favour of small and medium sized enterprises and the integration of the Common Market.

Although the different pedigrees of the labour market on the one hand and the goods and services markets on the other should not affect the principles applied, they do mean that a radical change in philosophy must precede the implementation of the changes necessary properly to draw that analogy. In essence, the analogy means that unless the normal market forces can be enhanced to change the nature of demand and therefore the practices of manufacturers and suppliers, both forces must be put aside and in their place a system of regulation and dirigisme must be instituted.

The pedigree of the two different policies, however, will clearly have an effect on the ease with which such changes can be introduced. Environmental paternalism of markets in which free competition has largely been allowed to reign will not happily be imposed upon the majority of Community industries.

It is not surprising, therefore, to find that the Commission in its Fifth Environmental Action Programme has not even hinted at this possible way forward. Instead it seeks to enhance its competition policy as a tool of environmental protection. The next section considers the specific application of EC competition law to measures taken by undertakings with a view to the protection of the environment.

4.7 COMPETITION LAW AND ENVIRONMENTAL PROTECTION IN PRACTICE

4.7.1 AFFECTING INDIVIDUAL ACTION

A preliminary point which should be made is that the focus of the discussion is on the activities of individual enterprises rather than public authorities. The question being discussed is whether the rules of competition law can be used to effect the way in which enterprises operate in order to take greater account and care of the environment when conducting their economic activities. Public authorities are included in their capacity as commercial entities in contrast to their capacity as administrative, quasi-judicial and legislative bodies.

4.7.2 THE STRUCTURE OF EC COMPETITION RULES

The principal Articles in the EC Treaty relating to competition are Article 3(g), Article 85, 86 and 90 and Article 92. Article 3(g) provides that one of the activities of the Community is to ensure that in the Common Market competition is not distorted. This is, in a sense, a general statement of principle which forms the bedrock of the more specific articles coming later in the Treaty. As explained above, the objective does not stand alone. Distorted competition is not to be attained to the exclusion of the other objectives of the Community. Nevertheless, the flavour of Community competition policy is clear; restrictions on competition should be reduced to a minimum.

Article 85 is concerned with agreements and other forms of collusion between 'undertakings'. Article 86, on the other hand is directed at the unilateral behaviour of firms which enjoy market power. Impugned behaviour is known as 'abuse' and market power is described as possessing 'a dominant position'. Abuse generally takes two forms: action intended to eliminate competitors; and exploitation of customers, end users and consumers. Article 90 is directed at public undertakings. It provides that they are subject to Articles 85 and 86:

"In so far as the Application of such Rules does not obstruct the performance, in law or in fact, of the particular tasks assigned to them. The development of trade must not be affected to such an extent as would be contrary to the interests of the Community."

Article 90 is important therefore in relation to the commercial activities of public undertakings. In many cases, such undertakings are granted special powers, even including statutory monopolies under national legislation. EC competition law challenges the possession of such exclusive powers in so far as they are unnecessary for the performance of the given public undertaking's fulfilment of its purposes and tasks.

Article 92 is concerned with State aids. The grant of State aids is, perhaps, more important in distorting trade than the creation of State monopolies. Typical situations of when State aids are granted are where politicians are subject to strong temptation and pressures to decrease unemployment in a marginal constituency by subsidising failing firms. Further, they can be used to give a 'leg up' to firms which have a strong environmental policy so that their more expensive products can be sold at or below their true costs. Article 92(1) provides that:

" ... any aid granted by a Member State or though State resources in any form whatsoever which distorts or threatens to distort competition by favouring certain undertakings or the production of certain goods, shall, in so far as it affects trade between Member States, be incompatible with the Common Market."

The following sections consider the potential environmental implications of the competition rules. A full analysis of each Article is given.

4.7.3 ARTICLE 85(1)

Article 85 is split into two distinct parts. This 'bifurcation' has been the source of much criticism particularly when contrasted with the 'rule of reason' approach found in the US anti-trust law. Article 85(1) lays down a broad and general prohibition on agreements that restrict competition. On account of its relatively clear meaning, this sub-article has been found to enjoy what is known as 'direct effect'. As a consequence it is automatically enforceable in national Courts and must be observed by national judiciary. Article 85(3) provides for the possibility of exemption from prohibition set down in Article 85(1). The Commission has the exclusive power to grant such exemptions. Article 85(3) is not, therefore, directly enforceable in the national Courts. This means that an agreement which infringes Article 85(1) cannot be enforced unless and until it has been notified to the Commission under the notification procedures set down in Regulation 17 of 1962 (the principal implementing Regulation for Article 85 and 86). The likelihood of an agrement being exempted under Article 85(3) is immaterial if the agreement has not been notified.

Article 85(1) provides that three criteria must be satisfied for an agreement to be prohibited. These are:

(a) a form of collusion between two or more undertakings;

(b) an effect on the flow of trade between Member States resulting directly or indirectly from the collusion;

(c) the object of effect of the collusion must be to restrict competition within the Common Market.

Article 85(1) gives a list of examples of violations of the prohibition. The list is not exhaustive, but in particular includes those which:

(a) directly or indirectly fix purchase or selling prices or any other trading conditions;

(b) limit or control production, markets, technical development or investment;

(c) share markets or resources of supply;

(d) apply dissimilar conditions to equivalent transactions with other trading parties, thereby placing them at a competitive disadvantage;

(e) make the conclusion of contracts subject to acceptance by the other parties of supplementary obligations which, by their nature or according to commercial usage, have no connection with the subject of such contracts.'

Article 85(2) provides that agreements which fall within the prohibition are automatically void. It should be noted, however, that where a prohibited restriction can be severed from the agreement as a whole, this will be done so as to save the majority of the agreement from the prohibition (see Consten SA and Grundig-Verkaufs GmbH v. Commission Cases 56 and 58/64 [1966] ECR 299).

Before considering the environmental potential within Article 85, the three threshold criteria for the application of Article 85 (1) are considered.

4.7.3.1 AGREEMENTS AND OTHER FORMS OF COLLUSION BETWEEN UNDERTAKINGS

Article 85(1) refers specifically to 'agreements between undertakings, decisions by associations of undertakings and concerted practices'. All types of arrangements are, in fact, covered whether legally binding or not. Further, the delineation between agreements, concerted practices and decisions of associations of undertakings, is blurred. Indeed, it is immaterial how a form of collusion is described. The law applies to them all in the same way.

Both horizontal agreements (agreements between competitors) and vertical agreements (such as distribution agreements) are included. Further, 'gentlemen's agreements' are also included.

Unilateral conduct on the part of an undertaking which is imposed on other undertakings in the absence of agreement does not fall within Article 85(1). There is not agreement on which that Article can bite. Instead, such activity may fall within Article 86 if the undertaking in question enjoys a sufficient degree of market power.

Nevertheless, the Commission has not found it difficult in the cases in which unilateral conduct has been argued to find some collusion between the parties, however tenuous. One of the Commission's favourite strategies is to find some continuing course of dealing or long-standing commercial relationship between the parties on the basis of which collusion can be established. See for example Case 107/82, AEG Telefunken v Commission [1983] ECR 3151.

The expression 'decisions by associations of undertakings' includes both the rules and regulations of trade associations which may be binding on the members and also the non-binding recommendations made by the association. Both the association and its members may be found to have infringed Article 85(1). Further, agreements between two different associations will also fall within the meaning of Article 85(1). Relevant cases include case 8/72 Vereeniging Van Cementhandelaren v Commission, [1972] ECR 977, Case 246/86 Belasco and Case 71/74, FRUBO [1975] ECR 563.

The phrase 'concerted practices' includes virtually any kind of knowing cooperation between undertakings. The Court's definition is:

"A form of coordination between undertakings which, without going so far as to amount to an agreement properly so called, knowingly substitutes a practical cooperation between them for the rules of competition."

(Case 48/49, ICI v Commission [1972] ECR 619. para. 64).

The notion is deceptively simple. It has proved difficult to draw the line between independent response to competitor's behaviour and concerted practices within the meaning of 85(1). The more concentrated a market, the more difficult the line becomes to draw. When there is a degree of similarity in the activities of competitors, the Commission's approach has been to presume that this stems from a concerted practice if there is no other explanation in the given circumstances. Parties under investigation should, therefore, be prepared to produce an alternative explanation of their conduct.

4.7.3.2 UNDERTAKINGS

'Undertakings' appears to have the same meaning in Article 85 and 86. It is a broad concept. It covers anything from a sole trader to an international group of companies. The key feature of any undertaking is that it carries out economic activities for its own ends. Employees are not, therefore, undertakings because they carry out economic activity for another. A group of companies is treated as a single undertaking. The nature and degree of link between companies for them to be treated as part of the same group have not been defined. Recent regulations and notices issued by the Commission refer to a link of 50%. This may not however be a precondition, and provided that one undertaking has control (for example by possessing a majority of votes cast at annual general meetings) over another, the two companies will be treated as a single undertaking.

The Court has endorsed the Commission's approach and in Case 16/74 Centrafarm v Winthrop BV [1974] ECR 1183:

"Article 85 does not apply to agreements or concerted practices between undertakings belonging to the same Group in the form of parent company and subsidiary if the undertakings form an economic unit within which the subsidiary does not have real autonomy in determining its line of conduct on the market and if the agreements or practices have the aim of establishing an internal distribution of tasks between the undertakings."

4.7.3.3 EFFECT ON TRADE BETWEEN MEMBER STATES

This precondition of Article 85 has been construed broadly by the ECJ and the by the Commission. The concept of trade covers all economic activities in relation to goods or services, including the right of establishment (the right of an undertaking to set up business in another Member State). Effects on trade between Member States need only be potential. In the Court's words the requirement is fulfilled 'where it is possible to foresee with a sufficient degree of probability that [an agreement] may have an influence, direct or indirect, actual or potential, on the pattern of trade between Member States'. (Case 61/80, Stremsel v Commission [1981] ECR 851, para.14).

What is more, the Community authorities are not concerned as to whether trade flows are increased or decreased. If an agreement affects the normal pattern of trade flows, competition may have been distorted and the authorities will wish to investigate. This motion is inextricably linked to the establishment and maintenance of a single market to which export incentives and import restrictions are equally divisive.

The Court has seen this criterion of the application of Article 85 as jurisdictional. In Case 56 and 58/64, Consten & Grundig v Commission [1966] ECR 299 it said:

"the concept of an agreement 'which may affect trade between Member States' is intended to define, in the law governing cartels, the boundary between the areas respectively covered by Community law and National law."

The Court went on to explain how the criterion is to be applied:

'What is particularly important is whether the agreement is capable of constituting a threat, either direct or indirect, actual or potential, to freedom of trade between Member States in a manner which might harm the attainment of the objectives of a single market between States. Thus the fact that an agreement encourages an increase, even a large one, in the volume of trade between States is not sufficient to exclude the possibility that the agreement may'affect' such trade in the above-mentioned manner.'

The effect of this approach is to include a vast number of commercial agreements within the ambit of Article 85(1). This effect is multiplied by the practice of looking at agreements as a whole rather than at their individual clauses.

Agreements confined to activities in a single Member State may satisfy this requirement. The agreement may be found to reinforce the compartmentalisation of markets on a national basis and therefore hinder their economic integration. In Case 246/86, Vereeniging Van Cementhandelaren v Commission, a Dutch Trade Association recommended the prices at which its members should sell in the Netherlands. The Court rejected the argument that because the agreement did not apply to exports, it did not effect trade between Member States. Even though the likely effect of the price fixing would have been to encourage imports of foreign cement at lower prices to undercut the Dutch traders, the Court was concerned that price fixing throughout the Netherlands would effect the pattern of trade between the Netherlands and other countries.

The very broad interpretation of this criterion by the Court and Commission has been narrowed slightly by the inclusion of a de minimis threshold in some cases. This threshold is often expressed by the requirement that there must be an appreciable effect on trade.

The Court's understanding of this de minimis requirement is expressed slightly differently from that of the Commission. In Case 5/69, Volk Vervaecke [1969] ECR 295, the Court introduced this threshold and indicated that the relevant factors comprised the turnover of the parties and their market share. The Commission has applied a more mathematical approach with its Notice on Agreements of Minor Importance. This provides that if the joint turnover of all the parties, including connected companies, to the agreement, or collusion, is not more than 200 million ECU and their combined market share within the Common Market or a substantial part of it is less than 5% then there will generally be no violation of Article 85(1). The Notice contains a proviso whereby the de minimis threshold will not apply if in the relevant market competition is restricted by cumulative effects of parallel networks of similar agreements established by several manufacturers or dealers. Clearly, therefore,in the area of distribution agreements the de minimis principle is of limited use. The Notice is not legally binding, although the Court in the context of tied houses has adopted a similar approach (see Case 23/67 Brasserie De Haecht v Wilkin (No.1) [1967] ECR 407; Case 234/89 Delimitis v Henninger Brau AG).

Regardless of their ecological content, the following is a random sample of agreements which may affect trade between Member States: (i) a joint selling agency agreement between competitors in which the agency pays its members the same price whether its goods are exported elsewhere in the Common Market or are sold on the domestic market. Agreements that reduce the incentive on members to export individually because the export price they receive through the joint selling agency will most probably be greater than they could obtain by their own efforts. Such an agreement therefore affects trade between Member States. Similarly, (ii) a joint purchasing agency in which the agency purchases goods on behalf of its members and requires its members to take a certain percentage of their purchases through the agency will affect trade between Member States. Owing to the fact that Members are committed to the agency to a certain degree, they are to that extent excluded from purchasing from other suppliers in the Common Market. Perhaps the most obvious example of an agreement which effects trade between Member States is (iii) a distribution agreement in which the dealer is prohibited from selling outside its defined territory. In EC terms, this is not necessarily an exclusive distribution agreement. An exclusive distribution agreement is one in which a dealer is given the sole right actively to sell goods in a defined territory. Where that right is shared with other dealers, it falls outside the Community's definition. Nevertheless, where an export ban is included in a distribution agreement it will have an effect on trade between Member States since the dealers' ability to sell elsewhere in the Common Market is curtailed. Distribution agreements in which the dealer is prohibited from selling to customers who are not resident in its territory but come into the territory to place their order will also effect trade between Member States. The freedom of the customer to purchase in the Common Market is limited to the extent that it cannot purchase in a given territory within the EC. A further example would be (iv) exclusive patent licences since their effect is to prohibit no one other than the licensee to produce the patented product in the exclusive territory, thereby reducing export potential. Clearly, therefore, agreements between undertakings involving economic activity may have an affect on the conditions of competition in any given market, regardless of their ecological potential. The agreement may be between competitors (horizontal) or at different levels in the production - cum - distribution chain (vertical). Provided that the parties are large enough, the first three preconditions for the application of Article 85(1) may be satisfied. Ecological arguments in this regard will largely be ignored.

On the other hand, there may be scope for raising ecological arguments against the fulfilment of the fourth precondition of the application of Article 85(1), namely that the argreement has as its object or effect a restraint of competition.

4.7.3.4 OBJECT OR EFFECT OF AN AGREEMENT

Article 85 prohibits agreements which have 'as their object or effect the prevention, restriction or distortion of competition within the Common Market'. An agreement need not actually restrain competition to fall within the prohibition of Article 85(1). It is sufficient that either the aim of the parties to the agreement is to restrain competition or, regardless of the motives of the parties, for the agreement to result in the restraining of competition. The Commission will consider the following aspects of an agreement when assessing its effect on competition. Firstly, it will consider that the objective of the agreement is by reference to its terms, taking into account the economic context. Secondly, if there is no identifiable anti-competitive objective, the Commission will consider the effects of the agreement on the market. The Commission will attempt to define the nature and level of competition in the relevant market in the absence of the agreement. The Commission's investigation will encompass the participants in the market, suppliers to and customers of the relevant market.

The Commission's approach is pragmatic. When considering the object of an agreement, the Commission need not consider the value of ancillary objects or goals. In Navewa-Anseau [1982] 2 CMLR 193, the Commission found that an agreement infringed Article 85(1) even though it had the ancillary objective of safeguarding public health and minimising the cost of conformity checks. When assessing the object of an agreement, therefore, the Commission is concerned solely with the economic context and not other aspects of the agreement. These come into play when assessing Article 85(3) exemptions.

The consequences for the ecological argument, therefore, is that regardless of the environmental benefits of an agreement, if the Commission finds that the parties intended to restrain competition in any way, the agreement will fall foul of Article 85(1). To give a hyperthetical example, if in a given industry, the participants voluntarily impose on themselves an anti-pollution standard for their products, and such standard increases their production costs by 10%, competition will be restrained since the parties have eliminated one important aspect of price competition. Further, since all the parties will be producing goods of a similar ecological standard, another element of competition will disappear.

The Commission does not find it difficult to establish an anti-competitive object to an agreement. In Case 19/77, Miller Schallplatten v Commission [1978] ECR 131, the Court referred to an 'optical and psychological climate' which can curtail competition. The mere presence of an anti-competitive provision in an agreement may be sufficient, therefore, for Article 85 to apply. The mere presence of the restraint, even if not implemented, will alter the parties' behaviour on the market away from the norm. An example might be where the parties to an agreement agree not to sell in each other's territories. Even if there is no sanction or implementation of this provision, its mere presence may cause each party not to intensify its sales within the other's territory. The conditions of competition prior to the agreement will therefore be altered.

The object of an agreement is determined not solely by the intentions of the parties but by an objective analysis of the facts. The economic and legal context of the agreement is important and is taken into account in the assessment.

Similarly, when assessing the effect of an agreement, the Commission adopts an objective viewpoint. Agreements can unintentionally restrict competition, therefore, and the parties may be completely oblivious. Article 85 will apply regardless. Nevertheless, the more unforeseeable and unlikely an effect of restraining competition as a result of an agreement, the more likely the Commission is to take a favourable view. The key for the ecological argument, however, is that the parties must not ignore the competitive effects of their conduct. In essence they cannot bury their heads in the sand merely because they are attempting to achieve environmentally friendly results.

Article 85(1) refers to 'prevention, restriction or distortion of competition'. The Commission does not distinguish between the concept of prevention, restriction or distortion. It has taken a broad approach such that any re-channelling or redirecting of goods from the channels or directions it would have taken in unrestricted circumstances is sufficient. Whether the effects are positive or negative is disregarded.

The Commission's definition of 'competition' is where arguments along ecological lines may be made. The Commission does not look for perfect competition in which the goods are homogeneous and market participants atomistic. Its ideal is a model of workable competition in which the following factors are important:

(i) Access to markets must not be unduly hindered by artificial entry barriers;

(ii) Changes in supply and demand should be reflected reasonably in the prices of the relevant goods and services;

(iii) Production and output should not be artificially restrained and should be efficiently flexible to move with demand;

(iv) The freedom of action of participants in the market should not be unreasonably curtailed;

(v) The choice of suppliers, purchasers and consumers should be unrestricted;

(vi) The opportunities for small and medium sized enterprises should not be unreasonably curtailed.

A number of specific clauses and practices often found in horizontal or vertical agreements are considered below. The list is by no means exhaustive. A choice has been made on the basis of their possible attraction to firms wishing to pursue an environmentally friendly objective in relation to either their production or distribution.

4.7.3.5 EXPORT RESTRICTIONS

An integral element of the Community's raison d'etre is the establishment of a single market within its boundaries. Market integration has had a strong influence of competition policy. Export bans and other restrictions which tend to divide up markets particularly along national lines virtually automatically infringe Article 85(1). The Court's competition case law bristles with statements similar to that in Case 19/77 Miller International Schallplatten v Commission [1978] ECR 131:

"By its very nature, a clause prohibiting exports constitutes a restriction on competition, whether it is adopted at the instigation of the supplier or of the customer since the agreed purpose of the contracting parties is the endeavour to isolate a part of the market."

This policy against market segregation applies to both direct and indirect restrictions on exports. Indirect restrictions include charging higher prices for goods intended for export, refusals to supply after-sales services in respect of goods bought from dealers outside the exclusive territory, prohibitions on repackaging of goods when different markets were accustomed to different styles of packaging and using trade mark rights to restrict exports.

It is clear that regardless of the ecological objective pursued by an undertaking imposing export restrictions, such provisions infringe Article 85(1). Justifications can be pleaded when seeking exemption under 85(3) but are rarely conceded by the Commission when applying Article 85(1). This bifurcation of the Article is unfortunately for two principal reasons. Firstly, agreements which infringe Article 85(1) are automatically void by the application of Article 85(2). They cannot be enforced in national Courts. Secondly, the Commission is the only authority with power to grant exemption under Article 85(3). Undertakings must tackle the bureaucracy in Brussels in order to validate their agreements. This process is slow and costly. Agreements which satisfy the conditions for exemption and thereby by definition improve distribution or promote technical progress, for example, in the eco-industry, are subject to an unnecessary series of hurdles. The process not only undermines the sanctity of contract, but it also slows down the speed at which new environmentally beneficial technology will reach the market and increases costs.

4.7.3.6 PRICE FIXING

Price fixing is another form of conduct which is treated severely by the Commission and Court. Unless trade between States is not affected, price fixing agreements always infringe Article 85(1) and are almost never exempted under Article 85(3). Competition in price is seen as the paradigm for a healthy competitive market. The Commission's abhorrence of such restrictions extends to retail price maintenance even when only on a national scale if it can be shown that trade flows potentially will be defected. Further, maximum or minimum prices are also within the prohibition.

Consequently, attempts by firms wishing to introduce environmentally friendly products onto a market by offering through their distribution networks low set prices will infringe Article 85(1) unless linked to a temporary introductory offer. Ecological products must compete on their own merits and not through anti-competitive restrictions. Once the polluter pays principle is fully and properly implemented, the restriction on price fixing will assist ecological products because by definition they should be cheaper than those products which are not able to fix prices to cancel out the effects of the polluter pays principle. Nevertheless, the polluter pays principle faces considerable difficulties of implementation and this restriction may slow down the introduction of eco-products.

Vertical price recommendation is acceptable in the context of franchising and probably is permitted in other types of distribution agreement provided that it is genuinely a recommendation and no kind of pressure is put on distributors to sell at these prices.

4.7.3.7 TYING

'Tying' is the obligation to buy both a principal and secondary product or service which by their nature or according to commercial usage have no connection with one another. Such a clause infringes Article 85(1). 'Eco-products' (so-called) are by definition, and in most markets, a novelty. This means that it will be difficult to rely upon some custom to justify the tying of a principal environmentally friendly product to other products or services which increase the ecological benefits. On the other hand, the benefit to the environment may be an argument which the Commission will accept along technical lines. Nevertheless, the connection must be genuine and the benefits must be empirically supported.

In a number of the Commission's block exemptions, obligations on dealers to purchase full ranges of goods are permitted.

4.7.3.8 CUSTOMER RESTRICTIONS

Within a distribution network, manufacturers of goods often wish to restrict the types of customers to which their resellers can resell. Within the eco-industry, this may be linked to a means by which undertakings without environmental policies are excluded from the distribution network in order to maintain the ecological reputation of both the goods and the manufacturer. Alternatively it may be a means designed to ensure that only those dealers or end users who can obtain the goods have appropriate methods of waste disposal. Other types of customer restriction include market separation into different types of end user such as institutional purchasers and high street buyers.

This may be because different after sales services and skills are required in relation to the various types of customer. Both direct and indirect customer restrictions are included in the prohibition. Consequently a clause by which the buyer agrees only to buy quantities needed to supply his own end user customers, thereby restricting him from reselling the goods to other distributors, will infringe Article 85(1). An example is Bayer AG OJ [1990] L21/7.

Reasons, ecological or otherwise, may be pleaded when seeking an exemption under Article 85(3) but appear to have little influence on the application of the prohibition in Article 85(1). Nevertheless, in the context of selective distribution it has been held to be acceptable in certain circumstances to impose certain limitations on the type of dealers to whom supplies may be sold. Furthermore, it is legitimate in selective distribution networks to require wholesalers not to supply end users. The treatment of selective distribution in the eco-industry context is discussed below.

4.7.3.9 EXCLUSIVE PURCHASE OBLIGATIONS

Exclusive purchase agreements require the buyer to purchase all its requirements of a given product from a single supplier. Exclusive purchase agreements infringe Article 85(1). They prevent the purchaser from buying elsewhere and therefore foreclose the market for competitors of the supplier. Clauses which have a similar effect such as non-competition clauses are treated likewise. This therefore prevents a manufacturer of an environmentally friendly product from restricting its resellers and distribution network to selling only environmentally friendly products. Obligations on the resellers not to sell or manufacture competing goods which have no ecological record will infringe Article 85(1). One argument that may be raised and which is explained further below is that the ecological product does not compete with its ordinary counterpart. Ecological factors are of a qualitative nature and make such a difference that the two products are not substitutable. Clearly, however, the Commission has not gone so far in it's definition of competing products although once the eco-market has been established there may be some mileage in this approach.

Exclusive purchase and non-competition obligations have been recognised by the Commission to have benefits. There is an exclusive purchase block exemption and non-competition obligations are accepted in the exclusive distribution, excluding purchasing and franchising block exemptions.

4.7.3.10 JOINT VENTURES

The range of joint venture agreements is vast. It includes joint purchasing, joint selling, joint research and development and joint manufacture. The Commission's approach depends upon the competitive relationship between the parties involved and on the nexus between the joint activity and the end market. Agreements between non-competitors are treated more favourably than those between competitors. The further the joint activity is away from the end market the greater the chances of a finding that Article 85(1) has not been infringed. Agreements between competitors for joint distribution will, therefore, virtually automatically infringe Article 85(1) and will rarely be eligible for exemption under Article 85(3) unless links to joint research or development and manufacture between the same parties and in particular where a product is highly sophisticated and requires sophisticated distribution. (Indeed, there is a block exemption for Research and Development, Regulation 418.85 OJ [1985] L53/5. Research and development in the area of Environmental Protection will fall within the scope of the block exemption. Indeed, statements within the Fifth Environmental Action Programme suggests that the Commission will extend its favourable approach to research and development to this market sector.

The Commission's approach to actual and potential competition has been strict. Potential competition includes undertakings which are not active on the same market but which have the potential to compete as a result of financial backup, technical knowledge and access to raw materials and/or technology. Joint activity between such undertakings will be treated strictly by the Commission. This will be the case even if the parties could not develop the ultimate product in the absence of assistance. Since 1983 and the Commission's statement in the Thirteenth Report on Competition Policy, the Commission has taken a more realistic approach to this aspect of potential competition. Where the parties can show that they would not have succeeded in the absence of assistance, the Commission will find that potential competition has not been restricted by the joint activity. Nevertheless, the Commission has continued to be inconsistent in its application of the principle. In essence, the new policy meant examining agreements 'ex ante' rather than 'ex post' as had been the previous approach. In other words, instead of looking at the argument with the benefit of hindsight, the Commission would attempt to wind back the clock and assess the agreement, the parties and their options at the time the agreement was made. In cases such as BP/Kellogg, [1986] 2 CMLR 619, Optical Fibres OJ [1986] L235/30 and Mitchell Cotts/Sofiltra, [1988] 4 CMLR 111, the Commission looked ex ante. However, in BBC Brown Boveri/NGK [1989] 4 CMLR 610, the Commission exempted a joint venture agreement which, if an ex ante approach had been made, should have been cleared rather than exempted. Prior to the agreement for joint development and manufacture of a sodium sulphur battery for use in vehicles, neither party had the full compliment of technology to succeed. The battery could be developed only if BBC Brown Boveri combined its battery technology with NGK's expertise in ceramics required for installation. In short, without the agreement the battery could not be made. Nevertheless, the Commission appears to have looked ex post and found that both parties were potential competitors.

Both the Fifth Environmental Action Programme and Article 130r(2) EC indicated that the Commission will take a positive attitude under Article 85(1) to agreements for research and development and manufacture of environmentally friendly products. It is hoped that the ex ante approach will be taken to reduce the number of agreements which are considered to restrict competition between potential competitors. It may be that one firm has the technical expertise and the other the environmental knowledge which, when combined, will produce an environmentally friendly result. Provided that it can be shown that the product either could not have been made without the combination of the two different types of knowledge and undertakings, or could only have been done so by incurring excessive cots and time, it is hoped that the Commission will find that Article 85(1) has not been infringed.

4.7.3.11 INTELLECTUAL PROPERTY RIGHTS AND "ECO-RIGHTS"

Intellectual property rights are part of the proprietary structure of national legal systems. As such by Article 222 EC, they are outside the scope of Community law. The Court has, however, drawn a distinction between the existence and content of an intellectual property right and the way in which it is used by undertakings. This distinction between the existence and exercise of a right has been severely criticised. Whatever the position jurisprudentially, in practice, a right is worthless unless it can be exercised. Similarly, the content of a right is in practice determined by the way in which it is exercised.

A typical example of the way in which the Commission approaches intellectual property rights is as follows. A trade mark may be used to impeded parallel imports by using a different mark for the same product in different territories. An agreement to use such rights in this way will infringe Article 85(1). One of the seminal cases in EC competition law exemplifies this approach: See Cases 56 and 58/64, Consten & Grundig v Commission [1966] ECR 299. In that case, a clause requiring the distributor, Consten, to use the trademark of the supplier, Grundig, on the product sold in France infringed Article 85(1). It had the effect of insulating the national market from imports.

The distinction between the exercise and the existence of a right has been combined in the Court's jurisprudence with the doctrine of exhaustion of rights. The exhaustion of rights principle states that given a specific product protected by an intellectual property right, once that product has been marketed and sold in the Community, the protection afforded by the intellectual property right is exhausted so that the purchaser can resell the product anywhere in the Community without infringing national intellectual property rights. The owner of the intellectual property right is entitled to obtain his monopoly profit once only.

Environmentally friendly products may be protected by intellectual property rights and therefore subject to the Community competition rules. The manufacturer may be able to obtain patents for his products or may wish to protect them by trademarks. By so doing, the manufacturer will be able to attain his monopoly profit either by keeping the exclusive selling right throughout the Community to itself or licensing them to third parties obtaining the monopoly profit through royalties. The intellectual property right licence will not in itself infringe Article 85(1) provided that it is not linked to an exclusive territory. However once an exclusive territory is granted and/or other restrictions are included in the licence, Article

85(1) will be violated. The same can be said for know how licensing and trademark licensing. The Commission has passed block exemptions for patent licensing and know how licensing. Provided that the eco-technology satisfies the national rules relating to patents or the Community rules relating to know how, the license of such technology to Third Parties will benefit from the relevant block exemption provided that the licence complies with the block exemption's provisions.

An argument has been put forward to suggest that the approach to intellectual property rights should also apply to eco-rights. (See Reto Jacobs, 'EEC Competition Law and the Protection of the Environment'). The suggestion is that at some stage eco-rights or the right to a clean environment will obtain the same status as intellectual property rights in the national legal systems. Should they do so, their existence cannot be attacked by EC competition law. A number of criticisms of this approach can be made. First, it is doubtful that the right to a clean environment will attach to any given product in the same way in which a intellectual property right attaches to a protected good. Purely because a product has features which are environmentally friendly will not confer on the manufacturers an exclusive right to sell the good and thereby obtain monopoly profit. Secondly, the approach ignores the distinction between the existence and the exercise of the right as drawn by the Court. Just as national intellectual property rights have been stripped of much of their content by EC competition law, so will this purported eco-right.

4.7.3.12 ACCEPTABLE RESTRICTIONS

There are a number of clauses and agreements which either have no effect on competition or have been held to be outside the prohibition in Article 85(1). Such clauses include the obligations to advertise, and to provide after sales and guarantees services. Other restrictions such as obligations to purchase minimum quantities or stock complete ranges of goods generally infringe Article 85(1) because they restrict the ability of the purchaser to trade with other competitors of the principal supplier. These therefore require exemption if they are to be valid. The approach to such clauses may vary depending upon the distribution context. For example in franchise agreements, such clauses as minimum quantities or stock obligations have been held to fall outside the scope of Article 85(1).

Two types of distribution system have been treated favourably within Article 85(1) by both the Commission and the Court. These are selected distribution and franchise. They are considered next before looking at the possibility of exemption in Article 85(3) on ecological grounds.

4.7.3.13 SELECTIVE DISTRIBUTION

Selective distribution is a distribution network made up of dealers selected at the wholesale or retail level or both on the basis of specific criteria decided on by the producer of the goods concerned. The dealers agree not to resell the goods to unauthorised dealers.

The selection criteria for dealers may be based on a variety of factors, including the dealer's and its staff's qualifications, the situation and appearance of the sales premises, the performance of before and after sales' services, the offering of repair services and guarantees, the willingness to engage in advertising and promotional activities and the capacity to achieve a certain rate of turnover. Clearly some of the criteria may be quantitative whilst others are qualitative.

The key feature of a selective distribution network is that dealers who have not been approved into the system by the manufacturer are prevented from obtaining the goods and reselling them.

Typically, selective distribution networks are appropriate for the distribution of quality goods of high value or technically sophisticated goods requiring skills in both advertising and distribution. Examples in the Commission's case law include jewellery, electrical goods and cars.

The main restriction on the resellers is a prohibition on the resale to unapproved dealers. Such an obligation has been held to infringe Article 85(1). Nevertheless, this is not a blanket restriction and certain types of clause have been found generally not to infringe Article 85(1). Most importantly, provided that selection criteria are objective and qualitative, clauses stipulating that non-authorised dealers may not be supplied have been found not to infringe Article 85(1). Clauses to the same end such as obligations restricting dealers to supplying only end users or other authorised dealers within the network are also permissable. Similarly obligations requiring the reseller to fulfil the supplier's objective and qualitative standards are also acceptable.

Nevertheless, selective distribution networks have been restricted by the Commission and by the Court to the distribution of goods which require specialised reselling skills. In essence, unless the type of goods involved merit special treatment, selective distribution will infringe Article 85(1).

An example of the Court's approach can be found in Case 26/76 Metro v Commission (1) [1976] ECR 1875. The Court stated that selective distribution agreements, provided that they operate on the basis of objective and qualitative criteria in the selection of dealers which are applied uniformly and in a non-discriminatory way to all potential dealers do not generally fall within the scope of Article 85(1). This approach has been frequently reiterated in subsequent cases.

Restrictions going beyond the mere imposition of objective, qualitative selection criteria and imposing other requirements do infringe Article 85(1). Consequently, territorial restrictions, price fixing and quantitative obligations are prohibited.

In the Metro (1) decision the Court held that selective distribution necessarily implies the obligation on dealers not to sell to dealers outside the network, as well as a method of checking that this rule is kept. Such monitoring obligations may include the keeping or records of all non-consumer sales and of proof that such buyers are authorised members of the network. The checks must be restricted to maintaining the selective distribution network and not to achieve some ulterior purpose such as the communication of price sensitive or market sensitive information.

Other customer restrictions relating to the type of customer may be acceptable. For example, provided that the differences between the customers are effected in different distribution needs, or different qualities of product, such customer restrictions may be permissable. An example from the Commission's case law is the difference between institutional china and the market for high street china.

Further, the Court has accepted that the different levels of distribution, for example between wholesalers and retailers, may be maintained. Consequently, wholesalers may be prohibited from selling to end users. The Court's grounds are that:

"If such a separation did not obtain the [wholesalers] would enjoy an unjustified competitive advantage ... competition would be distorted if wholesalers, whose costs are in general proportionally lighter because of the marketing stage at which they operate, competed with retailers at the retail stage, in particular on suppliers to private customers." (Metro (1), para. 29).

Selective distribution agreements which on their own would escape Article 86(1) may fall within the prohibition where the relevant market includes a large number of such systems run by the competing manufacturer. In Metro (1) the Court indicated that a selective distribution system might infringe Article 85(1) if:

" ... in particular as the result of an increase in selective distribution networks of a nature similar to (the present), self-service wholesale traders were in fact eliminated as distributors on the market in electronic equipment for leisure purposes."

(para.50)

The decisive factor is the effect of the network and systems in the relevant market. Where other forms of distribution continue to exist in the market, so that wholesalers and retailers outside the various selective distribution networks can obtain the goods for resale, the likelihood is that any given selective distribution system would escape Article 85(1).

The key question with regard to eco-products is whether they qualify for selective distribution treatment. In a number of cases and decisions it has been said that it is necessary 'to consider whether the character of the product in question necessitates a selective distribution system in order to preserve its quality and ensure its proper use'. (Case 31/80 L'Oreal v De Nieuwe AMCK [1980] ECR 3775, at para. 16). Typically, quality goods of high value and technical goods which require considerable after sales service skills necessitate selective distribution. Examples from case law of the Commission and that of the Court include televisions, radios and tape recorders, perfume, photographic equipment, high quality clocks and watches, personal computers, newspapers, cars, jewellery, high quality china tableware and ornaments and dental supplies including artificial teeth.

A number of factors are taking into account when considering the characteristics of any given product. In addition to their own inherent qualities, which may require specialist skills in before and after sales service, domestic rules governing entry to the retail trade or the conditions of sale of the product in question must be taken into account when such rules ensure that the distribution of the products in question is carried out with the appropriate skill and care. This might well be the case for goods such as medicines or firearms, for example. In the context of eco-products, the development of rules relating to the manufacture, distribution, resale and disposal of goods for the protection of the environment may render selective distributions unnecessary and therefore unjustified.

There is clearly an argument as concern for the protection of the environment increases, that products for which environmental friendliness is essential in the manufacture and marketing stages, should be found to necessitate resale by dealers who can demonstrate a high level of environmental performance. Just as the mechanical complexity of motor cars merit selective distribution, so the environmental qualities of an eco-product should merit distribution by environmental specialists. Clearly, hypertheticals are of little use and for the vast majority of products although some eco-marketing tool may be both appropriate and helpful, this will be insufficient to convince the Commission that selective distribution is necessary. In the more technical and complex types of products, however, this argument may well succeed.

Having overcome the hurdle of the nature of the product, the supplier setting up a selective distribution system must be careful only to adopt qualitative criteria when selecting its dealers. In the suggested example above, one qualitative criteria may be the environmental performance of the given dealers. This may include their success in environmental auditing. Such a criterion is clearly objective and provided it is applied without discrimination it should pass the Metro (1) test.

To assist in the selection of objective qualitative criteria, the following can be distilled from the cases and decision of the Court and the Commission:

(1) Criteria relating to the technical or professional training or qualifications required of the dealer or of his staff (Metro (1)) - for example environmental or ecologically based qualifications;

(2) Criteria relating to the type of equipment and installations available on the premises of the sale outlet (Metro (1)) - for example by requiring the selective dealer only to purchase products with eco-labels;

(3) Criteria stipulating minimum quality levels in respect of materials or equipment used in servicing or after sales care, regardless of whether the materials or equipment are available from the manufacturer or supplier or not (D'Ieteren Motor Oils OJ [1991] L20/42) - such quality levels could relate again to the environmental effects of the products used;

(4) Criteria requiring the goods to be sold in a specialised shop or in a specialised department of a larger shop and requiring separate display and an attractive setting (Villeroy & Boch [1988] 4 CMLR 461). The selective distributor may therefore be required to emphasise the environmental consequences of the product sold in keeping with the image of the products;

(5) Criteria imposing an obligation to take minimum suppliers, keep minimum stocks and display a certain range of goods. (Villeroy & Boch) - Such criteria, although apparently quantitative, are accepted provided that they do not constitute a large proportion of the dealer's capacity. Such criteria can be applied to all sorts of goods and may not have a specific ecological or environmentally friendly basis;

(6)Criteria requiring the sales outlets to have a certain appearance (Junghans [1977] 1 CMLR D82) - for example by requiring the prem ies to be predominantly green or to emphasise the environmentally friendliness of the products.

(7) Criteria obliging the provision of after sales service and repairs and the fulfilling of guarantees (provided that such obligations relate to all purchases of the products regardless of where the goods was bought) (IBM [1984] 2 CMLR 342) - such criteria relates specifically to the type of product concerned. Nevertheless, examples relating to eco-products include obligations to recycle waste produced by the product and returned by the customer, to dispose of waste and packaging in particular ways when returned by the customer, to service products at regular intervals to ensure that they continue to operate to a given environmental standard and so on.

(8) Criteria requiring potential dealers to furnish evidence of financial means and qualifications (IBM).

It must always be remembered that the qualitative criteria chosen relate to the requirements of the product concerned. If there is no necessity for a given criteria to be satisfied by a potential dealer, it will be unnecessarily restrictive and violate Article 85(1).

So far, the discussion has concerned Article 85(1). A number of clauses that may be individually exempted under Article 85(3) in the context of selected distribution agreements are considered below.

4.7.3.14 FRANCHISING

A second type of distribution system which may be appropriate for eco-products is franchising. Franchising allows a manufacturer or supplier to set up a network of legally or financially independent distributors which has an outward appearance of uniformity through the network.

The system has advantages for both the supplier (the franchisor) and the dealer (the franchisee). The franchisor is able to compromise on the one hand the expense and risk of setting up a number of sales' outlets himself and on the other hand loss of control involved in disputing his goods through completely independent distributors. For the franchisor it means that he is able to expand his network very quickly without substantial capital outlay. For the franchisee he has the opportunity to take advantage of an already well-known name and image and often gains the practical and technical help that the franchisor can give in setting up and running a new business.

This distribution formula is used for a wide variety of goods and services. Unlike selective distribution there is no qualitative content requirement inherent in the goods themselves.

In EC law there is but one significant judgment by the Court in the area of franchising. There are a number of Commission decisions and a block exemption which are based significantly on the Court's approach.

The Community's approach to franchising has not extended

beyond distribution franchises. Manufacturing franchises are not included. The key to a distribution franchise is that the franchisor has developed a well known name and appearance for its product often including intellectual property rights and know how. The franchisee adopts the product's and manufacturer's image but is financially and legally independent. Unlike an agent, the franchisee bears the distribution risks. Because of the benefits to the dealer in using a well known name and gaining in valuable sales expertise, franchising is often seen by the Court and Commission as a marketing formula particularly advantageous to small and medium sized enterprises. Falling within this policy area, therefore, it is not surprising to find that the approach has been favourable.

Since the formula is not limited to any particular type of good, it is one which may be used for eco-products. In particular, as the market responds to more environmentally friendly products and particular brand names and images, manufacturers will be able to enhance the market by using a franchise system of distribution.

The application of Article 85(1) to franchise agreements follows the usual approach with regard to territorial exclusivity and price fixing. The Court in the seminal judgment, Case 161/84 Pronuptia v Irmgrad Schillgalis [1986] ECR 353, stated that an exclusive territory when combined with a location clause granted to a franchisee infringed Article 85(1). It is probable that an exclusive territory even without a location clause will be prohibited. The key, however, of the franchise context is that such an exclusive territory even with a location clause is likely to be exempted under Article 85(3). The Commission has adopted the same approach to territorial exclusivity in a number of its decisions: Yves Rocher [1988] 4 CMLR 592 and Computerland [1989] 4 CMLR 259. Nevertheless, it is common to find exclusive territories within the franchise agreement. In the absence of exclusivity a potential franchisee is often not prepared to make the necessary investment in setting up and equipping the outlet. Consequently, the franchisee is often allotted a territory in which he is assured that no other undertaking, including the franchisor, will either have or be granted the right to exploit the franchise. The franchise is often required only to operate the franchise from a location specified in the contract and not to change location or open a second outlet without consent. The reason for this is for the franchisor to maintain a degree of control over the absence of the outlet.

In light of the fact that the grant of an exclusive territory is often essential to the establishment of a franchise network, it is unfortunate that the Commission has not taken a more realistic approach under Article 85(1) when assessing franchise agreements. The Court's judgment in Pronuptia indicated that in certain circumstances an exclusive territory may not infringe Article 85(1). In particular, it stated that only when such an exclusive territory combined with a location clause and when the franchise concerns a business symbol which is already well known would the restriction involved in the exclusive territory be such as to infringe Article 85(1). Further, the Court suggested that both the surrounding economic circumstances and the structure of the market should be taken into account in deciding whether a clause has restrictive effect. The Commission has done little more than pay lip service to any of these preconditions. Consequently, franchise agreements are sufficiently large to infringe Article 85(1) which will require exemption.

Other restrictive clauses may be included in a franchise agreement and any one will cause the agreement to require exemption. These include non-competition clauses, customer restrictions (for example preventing the franchisee from selling to distributors outside the franchise network), stocking requirements, active promotional obligations, and obligations to sell only goods which satisfy minimum objective quality specifications laid down by the franchisor or where such specifications cannot be set down, exclusive purchasing obligations.

There are a number of clauses often found in franchise agreements which do not infringe Article 85(1). Typically these relate to the protection of the franchisor's intellectual property rights and image. These include the following:

(1) The right of the franchisor to select its franchisees and their managers - this must not be used as an indirect way of restricting competition - for example, by choosing only those franchisees who will maintain certain prices for the goods.

(2) An obligation on the franchisee to apply the business and trading methods developed by the franchisor and to use the know how and industrial property rights provided by the franchisor.

(3) An obligation on the franchisee to use the franchisor's know how, trade marks, trade names and other industrial property rights in a manner in keeping with their subject matter.

(4) An obligation on the franchisee not to use the franchisor's trade marks, trade names or other identifying marks anywhere other than at the agreed franchise location and to stop using them after the termination of the contract - however an ex-franchisee must be free to use its own innovations or improvements developed during the term of the franchise provided that these are separable from the franchise system;

(5) An obligation on the franchisee to devote his best efforts to the operation of the franchise outlet and not to carry on activities incompatible with being a franchisee;

(6) An obligation on the franchisee to use for the sales outlet the layout and decor, both interior and exterior, required by the franchisor;

(7) An obligation on the franchisee to exploit the franchise from a particular location and not to change that location without the franchisor's consent;

(8) An obligation on the franchisee to submit to inspections of the outlet, including checking of stock levels, accounts and balance sheets - this must be restricted to checking that the franchise system is properly working, and not be used as an indirect means of restricting competition for example, by ensuring that recommended prices are maintained;

(9) A right in the franchisor to recommend retail prices. In the context of a franchising agreement this has been held not to infringe Article 85(1) - see para.5 of the Court's judgment in Pronuptia and in para.51 of the Commission's decision in Yves Rocher. Nevertheless, there must be no pressure on the franchisee to maintain such prices.

In addition, there are a number of clauses which have no competitive relevance at all. These are clearly outside the scope of Article 85(1). They include an obligation on the franchisee to pay royalties for any intellectual property rights or know how transferred (subject to the usual rule that such royalties must be earned and not linked to unprotected goods). They also include an obligation on the franchisee to assume a particular legal form, for example, an incorporated company; an obligation on the franchisee to indicate its independent status - this is seen by the Court as a measure of consumer protection; an obligation on the franchisee to take out insurance covering its civil liability and employers' liability during the term of the contract.

As can be seen from the clauses which are either outside the scope of Article 85(1) or are considered not to be restrictive of competition, there is considerable scope in the franchise context for protecting the ecological benefits of a particular good when being distributed. The manufacturer can select its franchisees against environmental performance. Further, it can ensure that the distribution outlet satisfies particular ecological standards. These may include obligations to dispose of waste in a particular way such as recycling. In addition, the franchisee can be required to assume a particular image consistent with the manufacturer's environmentally friendly reputation.

Because of the benefits inherent in franchise agreements, the Commission has passed a block exemption, Regulation 4087/88 (OJ [1988] L359/46) which grants automatic exemption for franchise agreements which satisfy the requirements set down in the measure. The block exemption is considered below.

4.7.4 ARTICLE 85(3) EXEMPTION

The bifurcated nature of Article 85 means that although agreements may be prohibited under Article 85(1), provided that it satisfies a number of factors set out in Article 85(3), the agreement may be exempted from the prohibition. There are four requirements to be fulfilled. These form an exhaustive list. All the requirements must be fulfilled cumulatively. There are two positive and two negative conditions. They are as follows:

> (a) The measure must contribute to improving production or distribution or to promoting technical or economic progress;
>
> (b) It must allow the consumers a fair share of the resulting benefits;
>
> (c) It should neither impose any restrictions which are indispensable to attain the objective of the agreement; nor

(d) Should it eliminate competition in respect of a substantial part of the products in question.

A number of preliminary points can be made. Firstly, it is clear that the agreement must offer objective advantages to the achievement of the aim set out in Article 85(3). 'Consumers' are not only the final users of the product but all persons who acquire the goods at any stage in their distribution. Consequently a retailer can be a consumer when purchasing from a wholesaler in the same way that an end user may be a consumer when buying from a retailer, and similarly a second hand purchaser from the original end user. With regard to (c), the notion of indispensability means that any restriction of competition must be conditio sine qua non for the attainment of the improvements mentioned in (a). In other areas of EC law, there is a notion of proportionality. This means that any derogation from rights granted by the Treaty must do the least damage possible to the right itself. The notion of indispensability in Article 85(3) is a parallel of the notion of proportionality.

Finally, with regard to (e), the specific conditions on the relevant market must be examined taking into account actual and potential competition between the parties involved as well as third parties. The notion of relevant market refers to those products which in the eyes of the consumer are substitutable, taking into account the function of the goods, their price, and their availability, and also it takes into account substitutes from the supply side. Supply side substitutability refers to those goods which can be interchanged by the manufacturer. Consequently, if a manufacturer can switch its production from making one good to making another without cost and time penalties, they will be regarded as substitutes.

Only the Commission has the power to grant an exemption under Article 85(3). In Case 127/73 BRT v Sabam (1) [1974] ECR 51, the Court held that Article 85(1) has direct effect. This means that national Courts must apply the prohibition to agreements which restrict competition within the meaning of that Article. On the other hand, however, the Court held that Article 85(3) does not have direct effect. This means that a national Court cannot grant an exemption and therefore must hold any agreement which infringes Article 85(1) as unenforceable under Article 85(2). This will be the case even if the national Court is clear that the Commission would have exempted the contract in question. Only if an agreement has been exempted by way of individual decision or block exemption, is the agreement fully valid and enforceable.

Agreements are eligible for exemption only if they have been notified to the Commission. Notification must be made on the appropriate form provided by the Commission (in most cases Form A/B) and that notification must be made by at least one of the parties to the agreement.

The Commission will apply the four criteria in Article 85(3) carefully. Nevertheless, its general approach is impressionist rather than scientific. Provided that the Commission approves of the economic competitive effects of an agreement, it will be exempted. Perhaps the most important of the four criteria is that the agreement be the least restrictive possible. If the Commission considers that a different and less restrictive method could have been chosen to achieve the same improvement or advantage, it will not grant an exemption. One criticism which has not yet been properly addressed is that this amounts to bureaucratic regulation of the market substituting hyperthetical s for reality.

This method of regulation may, however, turn to the advantage of environmental protection. If ecological factors are taken into account when granting an exemption the market may be turned albeit artificially in favour of environmentally friendly products. Some potential arguments which may be raised in relation to exemption under each of the four criteria are discussed in the next section.

4.7.4.1 ENVIRONMENTAL PROTECTION AS A REASON FOR EXEMPTION UNDER ARTICLE 85(3)

As explained above, as Community law now stands, positive ecological effects associated with an agreement are insufficient to qualify alone for exemption under Article 85(1). Further, although the Commission is under an obligation by reason of Article 130r(2) to integrate environmental policy into its application of Article 85, positive ecological effects are not again alone sufficient to merit exemption under Article 85(3). Nevertheless, the Commission must take such effects into account when considering exemption. In essence, where the other conditions of that Article are fulfilled, the fact that an agreement has positive ecological impact can be taken into account in favour of granting an exemption.

4.7.4.2 FIRST POSITIVE REQUIREMENT: IMPROVING PRODUCTION OR DISTRIBUTION OR PROMOTING TECHNICAL OR ECONOMIC PROGRESS

Positive ecological impact of an agreement may be taken into account in relation to the fulfilment of this requirement.

In determining whether improvements or promotion exist by virtue of an agreement, the Commission objectively compares the situation that exists with that in the absence of the agreement. Comparing the absolute with the hyperthetical is obviously imprecise. Consequently, the Commission is satisfied with a reasonable probability of improvements or promotion.

The Commission's starting point is that the forces present in a free market ensure improvements more effectively than restrictive agreements do. The onus on parties of an agreement is, therefore, to convince the Commission that the agreement de facto improves upon free market forces. The parties subjective assertions are immaterial. This was confirmed by the Court in Consten & Grundig v Commission. Further, the improvements must be to the market as a whole and not solely to the position of the parties.

From the case law, a number of factors have emerged as being important. Some of the more pertinent to environmental issues are discussed below.

Agreements which result in a reduction of costs and which allow the benefits of reduced costs to be passed on to consumers by lower prices are considered favourable. Once the polluter pays principle has been established, therefore, any agreement which adheres to the principle by reducing pollution will receive a position response. Costs may be saved in numerable ways. Those with particular ecological benefit include reduced use of raw materials, energy saving, recycling, reduced marketing and advertising expenses (for example by emphasising the ecological aspect instead of other less tenable aspects) and so on. The parties must establish that the improvement is substantial and that it is not superficial.

Another factor is improvement in the quality of the product. This was confirmed by the Commission in Yves St Laurent Parfumes OJ [1992] L12/24. Clearly this is an extension of the specific requirements in Article 85(3) but may have beneficial effects for ecological aspects of a product which contribute to its overall quality. As demand begins to respond to the ecological and environmental consequences of any given product, so the ecological record of a product will become an important factor of competition. Indeed, it may rank in the future along with the importance of price. In the perfume cases, the Commission accepted that differences in price of any given product may have an effect on its quality. For example, perfumes with a cheap price tag are often not considered to be of the same quality as those with both a known brand name and the corresponding bump-up in price. If price itself can effect the quality of a product, there must be arguments that ecological benefits of any given product should effect its quality in the eyes of the market and demand. This will be particularly so if it can be shown that demand moves with the ecological consequences and/or record of any product.

This approach to the characterisation of products has been confirmed by the instruction of the eco-label scheme under Council Regulation 880/92 of 23 March, 1992, OJ [1992] L99/1. The purpose of the eco-label scheme is to give a reliable indication to consumers of the ecological benefits of a product bearing the label. The label is awarded on the basis of criteria established by ecological and industrially based committees. These committees are required to take into account the effect of a product from 'its cradle to its grave' on the environment when setting the criteria by which the label is awarded. Consequently the eco-label gives and indication of the effects on the environment of the raw materials used, production processes utilised, method of consumption, and ways of disposal of any given product bearing the label. Such a system would not be adopted if it was not intended to have an effect on demand. Effects on demand will have a bearing on the price of a product and in the terms of the market on its quality.

Consequently, the Commission intends that a product with low environmental harm will be considered by the consumer to be more desirable and, therefore, have a higher quality, than products which damage the environment.

Agreements between undertakings which have the effect of improving the environmental record of any product should therefore be considered to satisfy the first requirement of Article 85(3) in a sense that it improves the quality of the product. As the eco-label system shows, it should not matter where the environmental benefits are achieved in the life cycle of the product: raw materials used;

production processes; energy saving; method of consumption; and waste disposal.

Another factor which the Commission has considered when applying the first positive criterion of Article 85(3) is what it terms as the 'broadening of offers'. This means expanding a market's outlook and economic activities. Consequently, an agreement which leads to increased diversity of product, new research and development potentials, increases in the number of suppliers to the market, expansions of points of sales, improvements and updating of procedures and services, improvements in transport and distribution, all satisfy the requirement. It may be argued that in addition to this list which is drawn broadly from the case law of the Commission and Court, should be added improvements in the environmental impact of any given product. This would not only increase the range of products available to consumers by providing another factor of competition and therefore choice, but will also satisfy the requirement in Article 130r(2), namely that the Commission should take into account environmental protection when assessing exception under Article 85(3).

The Commission has indicated its desire that new markets should be opened up. Again this falls under the first positive criterion. There are clearly improvements in distribution and also promotion of economic progress. Clearly, the institution and development of eco industry and eco products should satisfy this criterion. This may be by way of joint venture or specialisation agreement between two or more undertakings.

Although the Commission does not adhere to it, the notion of a perfect market entails perfect knowledge by all participants, whether suppliers or buyers of the conditions, prices, and terms available on the market. The perfect model is counterbalanced by the need to ensure that competition does exist. Competition frequently requires some degree of opacity. Indeed, transparency improving agreements tend to require the transfer of market and price sensitive information which when crossing between competitors can have a negative effect on competition. If one competitor knows the prices at which another undertaking in the market is selling its products including any hidden rebates, it will attempt to follow suit and will have the incentive to sell at a similar price, particularly when there is agreement between the two undertakings to keep each other informed. Nevertheless, the Commission may be convinced that greater knowledge in the market relating to the ecological benefits of any given product or service is a benefit which should be acknowledged within the first positive criterion of Article 85(3).

The Commission has adopted particular stances in relation to the various specific types of agreement. The categorization of different types of agreements correlates to the block exemptions already enacted, although there are additional categories which are considered below. With respect to exclusive dealing agreements, the Commission looks for improvements in distribution, enhanced penetration of foreign markets, improved after-sales' services, adequate stocking of spare parts, continuous supply, and the overcoming of legal and linguistic problems associated with foreign markets. These factors follow from the Court's decision in Consten & Grundig and the 1983/84 block exemption. Of particular interest to producers of ecological goods, enhanced by exclusive distribution agreements, are the possibilities of requiring dealers not to sell competing goods. Instead they should concentrate on ecologically beneficial products, exclusively to purchase the goods from the manufacturers enforcing the image, to sell the contract goods under trademarks or packed and presented as specified by the supplier, again ensuring that a particular image is established and to take sales promotion measures including advertising, maintaining a sales network or stock of goods, providing customer and guarantee services and employing trained staff.

In the case of selective distribution systems, the Commission looks for expert dealers able to market effectively a supplier's products with adequate demonstration, storage and general advertising space. The benefits of such a distribution method in relation to ecological products has already been explained. Clearly, provided that the ecological nature of the product is sufficient to single it out as meriting selective distribution, the benefits for the producer are obvious. Similarly, for the consumer, he or she will be able to benefit from the before and after sales service provided by the selective distributor and therefore enjoy an increased level of environmental protection. This will be particularly so if the after sales service extends to disposal of the product once its life cycle comes to an end. With regard to licensing agreements, the Commission's approach has been to look at specific clauses rather than to consider the agreement as a whole. The key to a licensing agreement is the conferring of a monopoly right. Such rights should, therefore, be exploited to their full. Exclusive licences whereby the licensor agrees not to grant licences to third parties in any licensee's territory, are considered eligible for exemption because they encourage the licensee to concentrate its efforts on the licensed goods. As a result the distribution of goods, including greater market penetration or opening of new markets, is increased.

Despite the benefits, the Commission will frown upon particular types of agreements because they have the converse effect to that sought in the first positive criterion on Article 85(3). In particular, export bans, price fixing, no dumping clauses, and prohibitions on customers selling outside national boundaries will almost never be accepted.

The improvement generated by an agreement need not occur immediately. Improvements may be derived in the short,medium or long term. In essence this does not matter. This approach is reflected well in the Commission's acceptance of research and development agreements which are, in principle, exempted from Article 85(1) and in which the results of research usually occur over a relatively long period. Consequently, although undertakings may agree to reduce their omissions or to improve their waste disposal activities, for example, the results may be reaped only several years hence. This should debar such agreements from exemption under Article 85(3). Provided that it can be shown that there is a reasonable probability of benefit to the environment in the future, the Commission should be satisfied.

When notifying such arguments, parties should put forward the likelihood that environmental standards will be tightened up and the polluter pays principle be implemented with greater effectiveness over the next few years. Agreements which seek similar ends should therefore be considered favourably notwithstanding their short term anti-competitive effect. Over a longer time span, the agreement should enable the parties to be in a position to offer products at a lower price than undertakings which start only after the new legislation tightening up standards or implementing the polluter pays principle comes into force.

Turning to other factors which may affect the application of the first positive critierion in Article 85(3) for exemption, the Commission has, in a number of cases, accepted higher safety standards in particular products as a justification for exemption of a restrictive distribution agreement and a restrictive horizontal research, development, and production agreement. In most of these cases, the safety standards related to specific products and therefore to the safety of identified consumers. Further, the causal link between the higher standard of product and the risk to the consumer without the enhanced standard was close. In the environmental arena, however, the risk is a more diffuse one, affecting people and their environmental as a whole and the causal link between the enhanced standard and the risk is more remote. Nevertheless, given the apparent priority conferred by Article 130r(2) on environmental protection, it is submitted that there is an argument by analogy with these cases to suggest that enhanced environmental standards should be grounds for the exemption of restrictive agreements which make such enhanced standards either possible or enable the dissemination and distribution of the resulting products. The following decisions are examples where higher standards have been accepted by the Commission in Article 85(3) decisions

In BMW, OJ [1975] L29/1, the Commission accepted higher safety standards in cars to justify an exemption for a selective distribution system. An indication of the Commission's approach can be found in paragraph 37 of the Decision:

"[Selective Distribution] can be considered to be a method of rationalising the sale and service of BMW vehicles and parts and thereby provides a better service to the Consumer than a system of free-marketing to which such cooperation is not detached. Motor vehicles, being products of limited life, high costs and complex technology, require regular maintenance by specially equipped garages or service depots, because their use can be dangerous to life, health and property and can have a harmful effect on the environment. It is therefore of importance that those responsible for the maintenance of vehicles are made aware of the latest technical knowledge which the manufacturer has acquired in the development and construction of the vehicle. Moreover, continual cooperation between BMW and its main dealers and retail dealers may assist BMW in the preparation of its maintenance instructions and training programmes, and may also lead indirectly to improvements in the design of vehicles'."

Although the Commission included dangers to life, health and property as well as harm to the environment in the BMW decision,it is submitted that the emphasis placed on environmental protection in Article 130r(2) of the Treaty means that products which threaten the environment may, for that reason alone, be subject to restrictive agreements to ensure that that harm is minimised or obviated at any stage during the life of the product. Clearly, the restrictions which may be included must relate to minimising or eliminating the harm. The principle of proportionality will continue to apply so that agreements which are not necessary for that legitimate aim will continue to violate Article 85(1) and not merit exemption under Article 85(3).

Consequently, in BMW, the Commission refused exemption to the selection distribution system because it conferred absolute territorial protection on dealers admitted to the system. This is unnecessary to achieve the legitimate aims identified in paragraph 37 quoted above. Once BMW had scrapped absolute territorial protection for its dealers, the agreement satisfied the first criteria of Article 85(3) in that it contributed both to improving the production and distribution of goods and to promoting technical progress. The Commission went on to find that the other three criteria of Article 85(3) were satisfied.

Notably, the Commission accepted obligations on BMW dealers to concentrate their efforts on the sale of and after sales service for BMW cars. These included restrictions on dealing in competing products without BMW's consent; limiting the number of dealers admitted into the selective distribution system, so far as such selection was based on the requirement by BMW of minimum standards for the selection and continued employment of dealers, and thereby ensuring that BMW motor vehicles were stored properly; that both maintenance and preparation and also services carried out under guarantee was sufficiently available; that any modifications to vehicles which become necessary could be carried out; that there was an adequate store of spare parts both in range and quality; and that technical problems found by BMW could be relayed rapidly and in full detail to the appointed dealers.

The arguments accepted by the Commission for an exemption of the joint marketing of nuclear fuels reprocessing services by a number of competing producers in United Reprocessors GmbH [1976] 2 CMLR D1, may be particularly useful when seeking exemption for restrictive agreements relating to innovative and new environmentally friendly technology. The Commission found that the horizontal agreement infringed Article 85(1) because its primary object was to coordinate investments relating to the reprocessing of nuclear fuels by the parties as a result of which each party was excluded from making any competing investment outside the programme. Further, another object of the agreement found by the Commission was to fix prices for provision of nuclear fuels reprocessing services because it provided for centralising within the joint subsidiary the supply of the services and the joint adoption by the parties of the marketing policy to be followed by the joint subsidiary. Despite these rather blatant restrictions of competition between the competing parties, the Commission was satisfied that the agreement should be exempted under Article 85(3).

In relation to the need for an agreement to contribute to improving the production or distribution of goods or to promoting technical and economic progress, the Commission accepted the following arguments:

(a) the agreement coordinated the parties' investments. This meant that uneconomic plants would not be set up and enabled the parties to wait until market conditions were most favourable before setting up high capacity plants. This reduced costs considerably because of the substantial scale effect in the nuclear fuels industry. Clearly, this is an argument applicable to new industries in which capacity is large but initial demand is small. The parties were able to gain technical experience and knowledge by coordinating during the early life of the market. Once demand was sufficiently large to sustain the paries operating independently, they were obliged to do so. Consequently, the agreement did not, in the circumstances restrict competition. On the contrary, it enabled a new industry to develop. The application to 'eco-industry' is clear. There may be new technologies and products for which the demand is small initially. If the risks are too great for a single firm to operate alone, the Commission may accept on environmental grounds coordination between competitors until the market is reasonably mature.

(b) A second argument was that the centralisation of reprocessing services improved the service offered to consumers by raising safety standards and by stabilising irradiated fuels reprocessing services. In essence, the agreement reduced the risks inherent in reprocessing. The agreement concentrated the points at which such reprocessing was to be carried out physically. Therefore, the Commission accepted coordination between competitors specifically for reasons of environmental protection. The fewer the points at which nuclear fuels reprocessing is carried out, the less danger to the environment. It should be noted, however, that the Commission accepted such coordination because demand for reprocessed nuclear fuels services was small. If demand was sufficiently large, the Commission would require the parties to operate independently from separate plants.

(c) A third argument accepted by the Commission in relation to the promotion of technical and economic progress, was that by combining research efforts, the agreement would help progress to be made as quickly as possible in the new branch of technology where further developments were still awaited on a number of points such as reprocessing of new fuels, transport and storage of waste, whilst at the same time helping to reduce operating costs and to improve the general standard of the service.

Clearly, again, there are parallels which may be drawn to 'eco-industry'. Where coordination between competitors will speed up the introduction of environmentally friendly technology, there is an argument for permitting such coordination because the Community is committed to improving the environment. To counterbalance such coordination, however, the Commission may look for reduced costs and/or improvements in the product. One would anticipate that such benefits would ordinarily accompany competitive coordination in a new industry. The undertakings concerned will often be putting their own existence on the line by undertaking such research projects. They are therefore unlikely to participate unless convinced, from a business point of view, that some benefits will be reaped in the market. An environmentally friendly market will operate in just the same way as any other. Reduced costs and improved products will be where the harvest is reaped.

(d) The final argument accepted by the Commission in relation to the information of technical and economic progress or the improvement of the production or distribution of goods was that the coordination in United Reprocessors enabled plants of optimum size to be built and worked with optimum mode factors. This meant that, at least in the field of nuclear fuels, the reprocessing industry in Europe could be made profitable. The agreement meant that the undertakings concerned would be able to develop their activities in the reprocessing field on a sound economic footing. Again, similar arguments can be made in the field of 'eco-industry'. New technology is by definition, a risky business. If by coordination, the parties concerned can put their activities on a sound economic footing, when if acting alone, the parties would be unlikely to succeed, the Commission may well accept restrictive agreements.

A similar series of arguments can be found in the exemption decision of Amersham & Buchler [1983] 1 CMLR 619. This case like United Reprocessors involved nuclear products. The Commission found that Amersham & Buchler were competitors. The agreement concerned was for the establishment of a joint venture to distributing in Germany nuclear products made by Amersham. The purpose of the joint venture was to ensure high standards of safe handling during transport and storage as required by radioactive products. In addition, the joint venture provided the basis for creating a waste disposal service for the radioactive waste of which most customers could not dispose of otherwise.

The Commission found that the agreement establishing the joint venture violated Article 85(1). It was a horizontal agreement between competitors to combine the distribution and sale of some of their products. The Commission's principal concern was that Buchler would have disincentive to expand its production to compete with Amersham's products having entered into the joint venture agreement.

Nevertheless, the Commission found that the agreement fulfilled the requirements for exemption in Article 85(3). Amersham was realistically not in a position to develop its products on the German market. A normal distributer of goods would not be capable of complying with the strict controls required for radioactive products. Again, therefore, the safety argument was accepted by the Commission. Further, German law relating to the transport and disposal of radioactive products were stringent. Buchler was an undertaking involved on the German radioactive market. It therefore had the expertise to provide the levels of safety required by radioactive products and was well acquainted with the relevant German law. The agreement, therefore, contributed to improving the production and distribution of goods since it enabled Amersham to enter the German market with a greater variety of products than before.

The Commission's approach to exemption in Bayer/Gist-Brocades [1976] 1 CMLR D98, provides a different line of argument which may be applicable to the transmission stage when environmentally friendly products are introduced onto the market. The decision concerned the formation, by two competing pharmaceutical companies, which were cooperating in the respective production of two penicillin products, of two joint subsidiaries controlled by the two parent companies through 50% cross shareholdings because the joint subsidiaries were a means of joint control and production and investment. When considering the application of Article 85(3) the Commission stated that an agreement must objectively constitute an improvement of production or distribution or promotion of technical or economic progress on the situation that would otherwise exist. A fundamental principle in this respect lays down that fair and undistorted competition is the best guarantee of regular supply on the best terms. Consequently, an agreement which infringes Article 85(1) and, therefore, by definition restricts competition is unlikely to satisfy the requirement of 'contribution to economic progress', except in those exceptional cases where the free play of competition is unable to produce the best result economically speaking. This will be in cases where, for example, state intervention or subsidisation of products itself affects the free play of competition. Consequently, in the market for penicillin (the relevant product in Bayer/Gist-Brocades) the Commission found that technical restrictions and difficulties limited the parties' ability independently to expand a production of the final product. Joint activity between competitors contributed, therefore, to economic progress which would not have been possible otherwise.

A similar argument could be made in relation to the markets for environmentally friendly products. At present, the incomplete and inadequate implementation of the polluter pays principle means that the external effects of environmentally damaging products are not fully internalised by the manufacturers concerned. In essence, such manufacturers benefit from a windfall by not having to take into account the cost of their pollution. Until the polluter pays principle and other environmental principles are fully implemented, free competition will lead to an inefficient allocation of environmental resources. Clearly, therefore, an argument can be put to the Commission that a restrictive agreement which reduces the cost of the manufacturer and distribution of environmentally friendly products by restricting competition between the undertakings concerned should, exceptionally, be granted exemption precisely because 'free competition is unable to produce the best result economically speaking'. Obviously, the circumstances of each market must be taken into account and it is not possible to give helpful hyperthetical examples. If it can be shown that the failure to internalise the external effects of environmentally damaging products hinders the introduction of environmentally friendly products, then restrictive agreements between competitors to assist in the development of such eco-products should, on the reasoning in Bayer/Gist-Brocades, be granted exemption.

A further point is that under the first criterion for the application of Article 85(3) exemption, in International Energy Agency [1984] 2 CMLR 186, the Commission exempted an information system operated by the major oil companies within the framework of the IEA. The IEA is a sub-body of the OECD. It operates an emergency oil sharing scheme for periods of crisis supply. This system only works because the major oil companies who are the principal carriers of bulk oil in the world are involved. It is the major international oil companies which will, in an emergency, undertake the redistribution and allocation of supplies pursuant to the agreement. When considering the contribution to improving the distribution of oil and to promoting economic progress made by the agreement, the Commission found that the object of the concerted practice was to reallocate available oil supplies equitably when it was in short supply. In essence, a crisis in supply would cause untold damage to the oil and other markets if free market forces were allowed to operate. Exemption was granted, therefore, precisely because the agreement prevented free competition from operating. It may seem a far-fetched argument, perhaps, but if the environment continues to deteriorate, parties to a restrictive agreement may claim that a 'clean environment' is a scarce resource which would be further damaged if the forces of free competition are allowed to operate. Consequently, agreements between competitors which aim to introduce products or services which do not harm the environment and which therefore seek to allocate the resource (a clean environment) more efficiently should for that reason qualify for exemption.

Finally, in a number of decisions, the Commission has accepted that enhanced environmental protection can improve production or distribution or promote technical or economic progress. In Carbon Gas Technology [1985] 2 CMLR 275, four companies which were originally undertakings belonging to major groups active at Community and international level in industrial plant construction and in the energy sector and therefore either actual or potential competitors agreed to create a joint subsidiary mainly for the purpose of developing to an industrial standard a process for coal gasification. Coal gasification is an alternative method of energy production to direct combustion of coal. Because the agreement restricted the competition between the parties and between themselves and the joint venture the Commission found that it infringed Article 85(1). Nevertheless, the Commission granted exemption. One argument accepted by the Commission was that the agreement assisted in the search for greater diversification and self-sufficiency and hence greater stability of energy supplied in the Community. Coal gasification would create favourable conditions through improved exploitation of Community coal deposits. Indeed, it was a more efficient method of energy production and less harmful to the environment than direct combustion of coal. National and other competent bodies associated with the energy industry had, prior to the agreement, repeatedly stressed the need for the Community to concern itself as a matter of urgency with the development of coal gasification processes. Since the agreement contributed to the attainment of such an objective, and most importantly, for present purposes, because of the beneficial effects on the environment, the agreement was found to promote technical progress and to improve the production and distribution of goods.

BBC Brown Boveri/NGK [1989] 4 CMLR 610 concerned an agreement between a Japanese company (NGK) and one established within the community (BBC) for the setting up of a joint venture for the development of sodium-sulphur high performance batteries. Although the Commission's analysis of potential competition between the two undertakings has been criticised as being inconsistent with its policy in the 13th Report on Competition Policy, the Commission granted an exemption under Article 85(3). The purpose of the agreement was to promote the development of high performance batteries with a high specific energy density. The intention was for their use in electrically driven vehicles and in the storage of off-peak electricity for use during peak load periods in national grid systems. When considering the criteria of contribution to the promotion of technical and economic progress, the Commission accepted that the cooperation between the two companies was aimed at developing a fundamental technological innovation which, by reason of the agreement, could be done more quickly and cheaply on a collaborative basis. The Commission stated with regard to electrically driven vehicles that the overall benefits were great:.

"An electrically driven vehicle causes no damage to the environment through harmful exhaust omissions or load engine noise. There is therefore much to be said for the cooperation agreement in terms of improvement for the quality of life of consumers for the development of batteries for vehicles."

This statement can be seen as an extension of the notion of promotion of technical and economic progress in Article 85(3). It is a specific example of the application of Article 130r(2) as it was at the time - that environmental protection should be a component of competition policy.

With regard to the use of high capacity batteries within national grid systems the Commission stated that as a result the output of the public power supply network need not be tailored to the hitherto peak load and a more economic use could be made of existing power generating capacity. Dependence on oil imports from third countries would also be reduced. Again, the benefits to the environment were clear.

The environmental dimension in Assurpol [1993] 4 CMLR 338 is clear from its facts. The decision concerned a French co-reinsurance pool covering risks of environmental damage. The Commission found that the agreement restricted competition within the meaning of Article 85(1) with regard to direct insurance because the participants were required (a) to cede business to the pool on the basis of core insurance premiums and (b) to apply general policy conditions formulated by the pool and pure premium rates fixed by the pool. Such provisions had a similar effect to exclusive purchase obligations and fixed prices in goods distribution agreements. With regard to reinsurance, the parties to the pool were required to reserve their reinsurance cover for their own direct insurance contract exclusively to the pool. Again this provision operated on similar lines to an exclusive purchase obligation and was found to violate Article 85(1). Nevertheless, the Commission granted an exemption. When considering the contribution of the pool to improving production or distribution and promoting technical and economic progress, the Commission considered first the nature of environmental damage risks. It found that the long time lag between the event giving rise to the damage to the environment, the occurring of the loss and the submission of a claim, and the lack of statistical data made environmental damage risks difficult to insure. The cooperation between insurance and reinsurance enterprises within Assurpol made it 'possible to improve the knowledge of risks, create financial capacity and develop technical expertise in insuring environmental damage risks'. Further, it enabled a more diversified and balanced portfolio for each of the pool members. The agreement also broadened the basis for generating statistics relating to environmental hazards. As a result, therefore, the pool enabled a more wide spread and effective insurance product for environmental risks to be available on the market.

The most recent decision is one reported in the 22nd Report on Competition Policy at para.177, VOTOB. The Commission's report of the case begins as follows:

"Although the Commission welcomes voluntary initiatives to improve the environmental conditions in a given sector, it has to ensure that undertakings competing in that sector do not resort to agreements which go beyond what is necessary to achieve that goal, to the detriment of competition."

Clearly, the Commission's approach in 1992, (in other words prior to the amendments to Article 130r(2) made by the Treaty on European Union), was that the requirements of competition should not be compromised by the needs of the environment. As explained above, this policy is likely to have survived the Maastricht amendments to the Treaty, although the profile given to the needs of environmental protection is arguably higher.

The decision in VOTOB concerns six undertakings offering tank storage facilities for chemicals in the Netherlands. VOTOB was an association of undertakings within the meaning of Article 85(1). The members of the Association agreed to charge to their customers a uniform fixed 'environmental charge'. This charge was to cover the costs of investment required to produce vapour emissions from the parties' storage tanks. The Association took this decision after concluding a covenant with the Dutch Government to improve environmental standards. The Covenant made no mention of a uniform, fixed price increase. There was no obligation on the Association by the Dutch Government to adopt one.

The Commission objected to the charge for three reasons. Firstly it was fixed. Regardless of their own considerations, each member had to apply it. Secondly it was uniform. Thirdly, by calling it a 'charge' the Association suggested that it was a statutory based cost. As a result of the agreement the Members had less incentive to make investments as cheaply and efficiently as possible. Because the charge was fixed they could not reap any benefits from such developments. Secondly, the uniformity of the charge meant that although individual members employed different techniques to reduce omissions with differing investment costs these variations could not be reflected in the charge, and therefore could not be extended to the market. Not surprisingly, VOTOB agreed with the Commission to renounce its fixed charge and to cease invoicing it as if it were a statutory cost.

The Commission concluded as follows at para. 185:

"The case makes clear that the Commission is not opposed to the possible passing on to customers of 'polluter pays' investment costs, since this makes them more aware of environmental problems and their implications. However, customers should not be debarred from challenging price increases and shopping around for the smallest increase. A system whereby members invoiced a total price, stating that it included the additional environmental investment cost, would be accepted to the Commission. Customers reluctant to accept a higher price would, far from being environmentally aware, remain in a position to negotiate conditions."

Undertakings wishing to propose environmental reasons for an exemption should not consider that environmental protection is a trump card before the Commission. In at least one case, the Commission has rejected environmental reasons for exemption. In Ansac, OJ [1991] L152/54, the Commission found that a joint selling association of American undertakings for the sale in the Community of natural dense soda ash infringed Article 85(1) and was not eligible for Article 85(3) exemption. It was clear that the agreement infringed Article 85(1). Its object was to require its members to sell soda ash for export to the Community exclusively through the Association, preventing them from selling individually, and therefore fixing prices. With regard to exemption, the Association argued that because natural soda ash was lower in chloride it was environmentally superior to many of its competing materials used in glass making, and therefore contributed to an improvement in the production of goods and to the promotion of technical progress. The Commission's retort was not to reject the environmental argument but to apply the principle of proportionality. It stated:

"Ansac's environmental argument ... presupposes that it is the only vehicle by which a natural soda ash could reach the Community, i.e, that if Ansac were not granted an exemption, no individual United States producers would market the product in the EEC."

The Commission had found that there was scope for United States producers to export into the EEC independently. The undertakings concerned were all large with sufficient trading experience and resources to provide their customers with a reliable source of supply.

The lesson to learn from Ansac is that the Commission will accept the environmental argument provided that objectively the agreement contributes to improving production or distribution or promoting technical or economic progress and that it is the least restrictive way of doing so possible. This means that it must not restrict free competition any more than is necessary to achieve the environmental aims.

Finally, with regard to the first criterion of Article 85(3) it is not necessary that the technical progress occurs at the same place or time as where the agreement has an anti competitive effect. This is implicit in International Energy Agency, Amersham/Bouchler, United Reprocessors and BBC Brown Boveri NGK. Perhaps the most explicit recognition of this possibility is in Ansac in which the Commission stated that the insurance pool covering risks of environmental damage was able 'to improve the knowledge or risks, create financial capacity and develop technical expertise' in insuring such risks, which in turn would facilitate the introduction of risk prevention measures and which would finally lead to the development of new production techniques less hazardous to the environment. The restrictions on competition at the time of the agreement were acceptable because in the future technical progress was expected in the goods and services market which generated the risks requiring insurance.

Further, in the Communication of the Commission to the Council and to the European Parliament on industrial competitiveness and environmental protection (SEC (1992) 1986 Final) adopted by the Council through Resolution of 3rd December 1992, concerning the relationship between industrial competitiveness and environmental protection, OJ [1992] C331/5, the Commission states that the voluntary activities of undertakings to protect the environment (which must include restrictive agreements) will increase the demand for eco-technology and accelerate technical and economic progress in the new eco-industry with its great potential. This appears to be a clear statement by the Commission that it will take a favourable view to the development of new technologies to prevent damage to the environment and therefore consider that they contribute to the promotion of technical progress of these products within the meaning of Article 85(3).

In conclusion, therefore, the Commission's decisions relating to restrictive agreements for both environmentally friendly products, and to other products, disclose a number of arguments which can be put to the Commission by the parties concerned when seeking exemption. It should, however, be remembered that the environmental argument is not a guarantee of success before the Commission. The Commission will continue to apply the proportionality principle and in so doing will assess the agreement in the economic, environmental and legislative circumstances. The benefits to environmental protection will be balanced against the anti-competitive effects of the agreement or concerted practice. The outcome will vary case by case. Nevertheless, the greater emphasis based on environmental protection in Article 130r(2) EC by the Treaty on European Union would suggest that considerable, if not primary importance should now be placed by the Commission on the protection of the environment.

4.7.4.3 SECOND POSITIVE REQUIREMENT: FAIR SHARE OF THE BENEFITS FOR THE CONSUMER

This requirement is not often considered at length separately by the Commission, because the kind of improvements required under the first criterion will normally be passed on to consumers if there is a competitive market in the goods. The argument advanced in this book is not that competition should or can be eliminated if environmental protection so requires, but that agreements by undertakings to produce goods or services which have beneficial effects on the environment in comparison to their 'non eco-industry' competitors, should be regarded as improvements and innovations which the Community requires if it is to progress. Such benefits therefore should not be prohibited simply on the ground that they result from restrictive agreements. In essence, such agreements should be permitted but should also be subject to the forces of workable competition. If this is the case in any given example, the Commission's usual approach to a second positive requirement in Article 85(3) should continue to apply.

Nevertheless, parties to such restrictive agreements may face certain difficulties in putting forward such an argument if their agreement leads to higher costs of production and, accordingly, increases in the price of the final products. The Commission's actual definition of 'fare share of the resulting benefit' is 'equitable participation in the resulting profit' (see KEWA [1976] 2 CMLR D15).

The primary advantage to the consumer is lower prices. When investigating whether cost advantages from restrictive agreements will be passed on to consumers, the Commission examines the state of the market. If the market is competitive the Commission is likely to conclude that there is sufficient incentive to ensure that cost savings and other economies are passed on. This competitive pressure may derive from direct rivals or from powerful purchasers who can exert pressure on suppliers thereby ensuring that goods are supplied on favourable terms. Alternatively, it may come from potential competition - competition from undertakings willing and able to enter the market. The presence of predators on the fringes of the market ready to pounce on any possibility of undercutting market participants or exploiting failures by existing participants to satisfy the consumer will also be a relevant factor. Potential competition alone, however, is rarely sufficient to act as effectively a disciplining force as actual competition.

Where the Commission finds no evidence of competitive pressures it is more sceptical of arguments that benefits have been or will be passed on to consumers. Nevertheless, the Commission will investigate the possibility that benefits in one area may outweigh losses in others. The fact that the Commission's list of potential benefits which may be passed on is not exhaustive corroborates this possibility. Benefits recognised by the Commission include: increased output to satisfy demand; improved customer services, guarantees and after sales services; regular supply and wider range of products; increased stocks; greater market transparency through more accurate and informative advertising; technical improvements in products and services etcetera. There must, however, be an objective advantage overall which is passed on to the consumer. An agreement which leads to a higher price of the product may qualify for an exemption if the consumer can benefit from other advantages such as increased quality. The increase in price must not be excessive or unreasonable when compared with the improved quality.

As has been explained above, there are considerable arguments to suggest that an improved environmental record of a product should be accepted as improving the quality of the product. Further, increased information relating to the product's environmental record should also constitute a benefit. The Community's eco-labelling scheme, which is aimed at providing the consumer with information about the product from 'its cradle to its grave', may be put forward as an argument to the Commission that improved transparency in the environmental context is a benefit which should be recognised in Article 85(3). (See for the eco-labelling scheme, Council Regulation 880/92, OJ [1992] L99/1). The argument is that if the environmental impact of a product can be reduced by restrictive agreements, the quality of the product increases and should therefore be justifiable under Article 85(3).

Another problem for eco-industry is that often their benefits which can be passed on to the consumer are generated over a longer term than the impact of their restrictions on competition. The Commission has accepted that such a difference in where or when benefits are received by the consumer does not in itself disapply Article 85(3). In Synthetic Fibres [1985] 1 CMLR 787, which concerned an agreement between producers in the synthetic fibre market to reduce capacity so as to overcome as effectively as possible difficulties created by overcapacity in the industry, the Commission accepted that consumers stood to gain from the improvement in the production in that the industry which would eventually emerge from the restructuring plan instigated by the parties. In addition the parties themselves would be healthier and more competitive and able to offer potential customers better products thanks to greater specialisation. Further, the agreement would ensure that the shake-out of overcapacity in the industry would eliminate the non-viable and obsolete plant that could only have survived at the expense of the profitable plant through external subsidies or loss financing within the group, and should leave only the competitive plants and businesses in operation.

Although the circumstances in Synthetic Fibres are the converse of the prospects faced by eco-industry, similar arguments may be made. The circumstances facing undertakings, researching, developing and producing environmentally friendly products to compete with existing non eco-technology goods, are similar to the future faced by the undertakings in Synthetic Fibres. Without some form of coordination, the companies in Synthetic Fibres could all fail. Similarly, without some form of coordination, eco-technology may not be able to get off the ground because of the risks involved. In both, therefore, consumers will stand to gain from the improvements in research, development and production, in that 'the industry which would eventually emerge would be healthier and more competitive and able to offer them better environmental products'.

This argument can be reinforced by showing that in comparison to undertakings which fail to develop and make investments in environmentally friendly technology at present, there are those undertakings which do make such investments, and that by employing a forward thinking philosophy to their businesses will be in a position to offer eco-products at a lower price in the future precisely because they have already adjusted to the new needs of the market and the Community. Consumers will benefit from restrictions applying today in the long run.

A typical argument put forward and often accepted by the Commission is that the parties have coordinated to produce products which would not have been viable if the undertakings had acted independently. This is the 'bird in the hand is worth two in the bush' argument. Cases in which this argument has been accepted by the Commission, and which have relevance for the environment, include Assurpol, BBC Brown Boveri/NGK and VOTOB.

Benefits conferred must be adequate. Article 85(3) requires that consumers have a 'fair share' of the resulting benefit. This means that so far as is practicable, the consumer must obtain a fair share of all the benefits perceived to flow from the agreement. The parties must, therefore, give consumers information relating to the environmental aspects of their products if such is the purpose of their restrictive agreement. Similarly if an agreement confers costs savings and higher quality produce or services, the consumer must obtain the higher quality product or service at a reasonable price which affects the costs savings.

The meaning of consumer has received a variable response from the Commission. In the early days, the Commission applied a restrictive view. Consequently in ACEC Berliet [1968] CMLR D35, the 'consumers' of a bus were held to be bus companies and tour operators, not commuters or tourists. An indication of the Commission's approach can be gleaned from the French text of 'consumers', that being 'utilisateurs'. This word means ultimate buyers rather than ultimate consumers.

Nevertheless, more recent cases indicate a change in direction and a broadening of the definition. First, the expression is not limited to end users, but includes users at all stages of production and consumption. In KSB Lowara/Goulds Pumps/IT [1992] 5 CMLR 655, the Commission granted an individual exemption to a joint research and development agreement between competing pump manufacturers for the development of advanced pump components. When considering whether consumers enjoyed a fair share of the resulting benefit from the agreements, the Commission reasoned as follows:

"The advantages arising from the cooperation benefits consumers at the very least through the improvement in the quality of water pumps. Moreover, two aspects of the new pumps, i.e. energy conservation and the fact that the fluids handled by the pump are not polluted, are environmentally beneficial. This effect is reinforced by the higher performance capacity of the pumps. This constitutes an improvement in operating characteristics. At least at present, a further advantage is that these pumps are offered to consumers at the same price as cast iron pumps."

Clearly, therefore, the Commission was willing to accept that the concept of 'consumers' was wider than the ultimate buyer. All persons using such pumps, and therefore consumers in a wider sense, would benefit from the improved environmental operation of the new pumps.

It is unlikely, however, that the notion of consumers will be expanded to the Community at large in the sense that everyone will benefit from a clean environment. There must be some direct link between the product and the person receiving the benefit.

4.7.4.4 FIRST NEGATIVE REQUIREMENT: INDISPENSABILITY

Article 85(3) provides that the agreements must not 'impose on the undertakings concerned restrictions which are not indispensable to the attainment of these objectives'.

This requirement is assessed objectively by the Commission. Given that the agreement has a legitimate aim (the first positive requirement of Article 85(3)), the Commission will investigate whether the agreement seeks to achieve the aim in the least restrictive way possible. Looking at the test from the parties' point of view, they must ask themselves whether they need all of the restrictions in their agreement. If the agreement contains superfluous and therefore dispensable restrictions it is likely to refuse an exemption. Frequently, the Commission will require the parties to modify their agreement.

One of the arguments suggested above is that parties to an agreement aimed at improving the environmental record of a product satisfy the first positive criterion of Article 85(3) in that they have thereby improved the quality of the product. This is a legitimate aim. The parties must then assess whether the restrictions they have imposed on each other are necessary to achieve that aim. This is clearly a difficult task since it requires the parties to prove a negative. Each case will turn on its own facts and circumstances. Nevertheless, in VOTOB the Commission accepted that measures to protect the environment can fulfil the requirement of indispensability when the measure does not go beyond what is necessary to achieve the goal. There it found that the criterion was not fulfilled because the undertakings agreed to charge their consumers a uniform and fixed 'charge' for the environmental consequences of their product. Such environmental benefits could be obtained without restricting the freedom of the parties to charge different prices and without calling the sum a 'charge' thereby suggesting that it was statutorily imposed.

The Commission does not accept arguments by parties that they would not have concluded the agreement without an impugned restriction. This is because such arguments are linked to the subjective views of the parties and not to the objective test applied by the Commission. A more reliable test applied by the Commission is whether a reasonable, hyperthetical businessman would have entered the agreement without the restriction. The more central a restriction is to the agreement, the more likely it is to be accepted.

Certain restrictions are generally considered indispensable to particular types of agreements. Exclusivity clauses in exclusive dealing agreements may be indispensable in achieving effective distribution of the supplier's goods. This was accepted by the Commission and Court in Consten & Grundig [1964] CMLR 489 (Commission decision). Similarly exclusive licences of intellectual property rights may be necessary to provide the incentive for the licensee to exploit the right effectively.

It should be noted that the approach to indispensability in Article 85(3) is different from the concept of proportionality in Articles 30-36. In the former Article, once the Commission has accepted the aim of an agreement to be legitimate, it will then investigate whether the provisions of the agreement concerned are necessary and indispensable. In Article 36, however, the Commission does not first decide that an aim is legitimate, but will balance the aim against the need for free trade. Consequently, in Case 302/86 Commission v Denmark (Danish Bottles), [1988] ECR 4607. the Court attempted to strike a balance between two competing goals; the need for environmental protection and the quest for free trade. It ruled that certain measures were not proportional and therefore incompatible with the Treaty because they were designed to achieve an unreasonably high level of environmental protection. In essence, the Court decided that the aim of the national measure was unacceptable within the Community scheme.

4.7.4.5 SECOND NEGATIVE REQUIREMENT: ELIMINATION OF COMPETITION

Within the terms of Article 85(3)(b) the agreement must not 'afford such undertakings the possibility of eliminating competition in respect of a substantial part of the products in question'.

As explained above, Article 130r(2) does not alter the application of this requirement. As with the first negative requirement, the second negative requirement is an absolute barrier to exemption. The Commission must define the product market. It is unlikely that the Commission will accept arguments along the lines that if a product has got environmentally beneficial results it should not be considered as substitutable and therefore in the same market as other products which do not have the same affect. Eco-friendliness is not a characteristic of such importance at present as to create separate markets.

The Commission's analysis focuses often on the market share of the parties to the agreement and the market structure. Parties who together control 60% or more of the market are unlikely to be granted exemption because competition outside the agreement will be under severe strain. Parties with 50% of the market may be granted exemption but must show external factors which will convince the Commission that competition is maintained.

At the level of 30% market share enjoyed by the parties to an agreement, effective competition can probably exist outside the agreement. Where the agreement has been made by small parties to compete against larger existing firms, the agreement may indeed enhance competition. Anything below 10% of market share held by the parties is unlikely to effect competition at all.

Market share is not necessarily the only criterion. Indeed, the Commission has stated that market share of 90% or more need not disqualify an agreement for exemption if exceptional circumstances obtain. In United Reprocessors three major reprocessors of nuclear fuels combined in a joint research, development and marketing cartel. There were considerable restrictions of competition within the cartel. Further, there was no effective competition in the Community outside of the parties. Nevertheless, the Commission exempted the agreement. It appears that this was because of the political need for the EC to have a corporation that could compete on the world market especially with tense US competition. There were explicit Community energy and environmental policy considerations taken into account.

Other factors besides market share which have been considered under the rubric of the second negative requirement include: the existence of intense competition on the world market; the need for restructuring to produce a healthier competitive climate; and the need for cooperation between the undertakings to produce a new strain of technology or good.

4.7.4.6 COMMISSION'S APPROACH

The Commission's approach is to negotiate the possibility of exemption with the parties. This will often involve the Commission imposing conditions on exemption. It may require the parties to scrap certain provisions or to undertake to inform the Commission of any regular specified information relating both to the performance of the agreement and the market circumstances. Whilst this approach has been criticised for undermining the contract law of Europe, it does mean a certain flexibility in the application of Article 85(3). It is at this stage that the ecological arguments should be put forward to the Commission. Parties should begin their overtures to the Commission on the basis of Article 130r(2) and the Commission's own statements in its Communication to the Council and European Parliament and the Council Resolution endorsing that Communication.

In essence, parties should suggest to the Commission that the amended Article 130r(2) has imposed a fifth requirement on the grant of an exemption under Article 85(3). The Commission should not grant an exemption unless it has taken ecological considerations into account. Agreements which hinder environmental protection should not be exempted. Agreements which improve the environment should, as explained above, be considered favourably. Although the approach will be a balancing act, the emphasis placed on environmental protection in Article 130r(2) will suggest that it will be difficult for an agreement which may result in considerable environmental harm ever to be exempted under Article 85(3).

4.7.4.7 BLOCK EXEMPTIONS

Under Article 85(3) the Commission has the power not only to grant individual exemption on application by one or more of the parties to the agreement, but also to issue 'block exemptions'. These take the form of a Regulation and are published in the 'L' series of the Official Journal. The block exemption will specify a number of pre-conditions which an agreement must satisfy. In essence, the block exemptions have resulted in a degree of standard form contracting throughout the Community. If parties take care to draft an agreement which satisfies the requirements of a block exemption and do not include any of the forbidden 'black listed' clauses listed in the relevant Regulation, they will benefit from automatic exemption without the need for individual application to the Commission.

More recent block exemptions have included a procedure known as the 'opposition procedure' which enables parties who have drafted agreements which do not comply to the letter of the Regulation but which do not include any black listed clauses to apply to the Commission for speedy individual exemption. Once the agreement has been notified to the Commission, the agreement is deemed exempt if the Commission then takes no action within 6 months.

The use of block exemptions is usually a far more attractive option than applying for individual exemption. The latter comprises a process which is neither time nor cost conscious, and often ends unsatisfactorily with the use of informal and non-binding comfort letters rather than formal decisions.

The Commission can withdraw the benefit of a block exemption from an agreement if it comes to the conclusion that, despite compliance with the requirements of the block exemption, the agreement does not fulfil the requirements of Article 85(3). This will often happen if competition in the market is lacking or customers are unable to obtain the goods concerned outside of the Agreement.

Five of the block exemptions so far enacted have particular relevance in the field of environmental protection; patent licensing, Regulation 2349/84; know how licensing, Regulation 556/89; research and development, Regulation 418/85; exclusive distribution, Regulation 1983/83; and franchising, Regulation 4087/88.

The first point to note is that although the Regulations are secondary law as opposed to the primary law in the Treaty, they are subject to the general policy requirements of the Treaty including Article 130r(2). Consequently, the criteria of the block exemptions must be defined and implemented taking into account the requirement of environmental protection. This should mean, therefore, that agreements which fulfil the criteria of a block exemption and which have environmentally friendly results should qualify for automatic exemption.

An example of this happening is KSB/Goulds/Lowara/IT OJ [1990] L19/25 The Commission accepted that research and development undertaken by the parties for the purposes of developing environmentally friendly water pumps fell within the scope of the block exemption because their cooperation was of commercial necessity in order to attain the introduction of the new product on the market. Nevertheless, the block exemption did not apply because it was highly likely that the parties would exceed the permissable 20% market share and would exceed the turnover threshold for the applicability of Regulation 418/85.

Where an agreement contains restrictions necessary to achieve environmentally friendly results but which are outside the scope of a relevant block exemption, it is submitted that the Commission should take the environmentally friendly results into account when considering the application of the opposition procedure to such an agreement. It should be remembered, however, that not all block exemptions contain an opposition procedure. Most importantly the exclusive distribution (1983/83) and exclusive purchasing (1984/83) Regulations do not include an opposition procedure. In the latter cases, the parties must notify their agreement individually.

Further, Article 130r(2) should, it is submitted, be interpreted so that agreements which have a considerable negative impact upon the environment should not be exempted under Article 85(3). This should apply similarly to block exemptions. Although Article 130r(2) does not amend the provisions of the Regulations themselves, the Commission may, it is submitted, use the possibility of withdrawal of the benefit of the block exemption on these grounds. If the Commission comes to the conclusion that an agreement which falls within a block exemption has a considerable negative impact upon the environment, which cannot be outweighed by the benefits, it should withdraw the exemption. Although this criterion is not specifically written into the Regulations, legal certainty will not be compromised because, as with all Community secondary legislation, it is subject to Treaty provisions. The basis of this argument is Article 130r(2) and therefore is consistent with Community law.

A brief resume of the relevant block exemptions follows.

4.7.4.7.1 EXCLUSIVE DISTRIBUTION

The exclusive distribution block exemption automatically exempts agreements in which a distributor is granted an exclusive territory for the resale of goods, provided that there are only two parties to the agreement. Having automatically been exempted from Article 85(1), the agreement may be enforced by the parties in national courts. There can be no complete ban on exporting out of the territory given to the exclusive distributor, but the distributor may be prohibited from taking active steps to market the goods outside his territory. The supplier may chose to supply certain end users within the territory but must agree not appoint another distributor for the territory. He may require the distributor not to make or sell competing goods. The exemption does not apply to agreements between competing manufacturers unless it is not reciprocal and at least one of the two parties has a turnover of less than 100 million ECU.

4.7.4.7.2 FRANCHISING

Franchising is a relatively new distribution method which is of particular advantage to small and medium size enterprises. It allows a manufacturer or supplier to maintain an outward appearance of uniformity whilst using a network of legally and financially independent distributors. Consequently, the supplier can expand rapidly whilst the dealers or franchisees have the benefit of the manufacturer or franchiser's know how and brand image. The block exemption exempts from the application of Article 85(1) franchise contracts between two undertakings which include one or more of the restrictions listed in Article 2, and, most importantly, certain territorial restrictions. There are a number of clauses set out in the block exemption which may be included in the franchise agreement either because in most circumstances they do not infringe Article 85(1) EC, or because in the context of a franchise agreement they are considered necessary. Article 5 sets out the 'black list' of clauses which will prevent an agreement from benefiting from the exemption. Most importantly these include price fixing, absolute territorial restrictions and agreements between competitors. The block exemption includes an opposition procedure which, as explained above, allows parties to notify agreements that would come within the scope of the exemption but for the inclusion of anti-competitive clauses (including those relating to the protection of the environment) not dealt with in the Regulation. If the Commission does not object to an agreement notified under this procedure within 6 months, the agreement is automatically exempted. Article 8 provides the power for the Commission to withdraw the benefit of the Regulation from any particular agreement. The following points should be noted. It is permissable for the franchisor to indicate recommended prices to franchisees but must not pressurise the latter to keep to such prices. Clauses necessary to prevent the franchisor's know how benefitting his competitors outside the franchise are eligible for exemption. Clauses necessary for the maintenance of the identity and reputation of the franchise network are also eligible for exemption.

4.7.4.7.3 PATENT LICENSING

The basic scheme of Regulation 2349/84 is that Article 1 exempts exclusive and some other patent licences. The white list of clauses that normally do not infringe Article 85(1) EC but are exempted just in case are set out in Article 2. Article 3 contains the black list of conditions that prevent the application of the exemption, Article 4 provides for the opposition procedure. The agreement must be made between not more than two undertakings and therefore does not apply to patent licensing. Further, reciprocal agreements between competitors, if there are territorial restrictions, are excluded. The patent licence may include other intellectual property rights provided that the patent is the principal element. Exclusive territories may be given to licensees in which the licensor agrees not to appoint other licensees or to exploit the technology itself. However, the principle of exhaustion over intellectual property rights means that once a licensee has marketed a particular good anywhere in the Community other licensees cannot prevent the resale of that particular good in their territories. Passive selling by licensees in territories other than their own can be restricted for a period of five years from the date that it is first put on the market within the Common Market by the licensor or one of his licensees. Black listed clauses include no challenge clauses, price fixing, extension of royalties to unprotected products, exclusive grant-back clauses and unnecessary tying.

4.7.4.7.4 KNOW HOW LICENSING

The know how licence block exemption, 556/89, is similar to the patenting licensing block exemption, although the periods permitted for territorial protection are different. Restrictions between licensee and licensor may last for 10 years from the first licence in the territory. Restrictions active sales as between licensees may last for up to ten years from the first licence in the Common Market. Protection against passive sales is permitted for 5 years from the first licence in the Common Market.

4.7.4.7.5 RESEARCH AND DEVELOPMENT

The Commission is not prepared to exempt joint ventures generally, since the criteria in Article 85(3) EC in relation to agreements between competitors is not easy to apply. However, it has exempted, by way of block exemption, a limited class of joint ventures for research and development. The block exemption covers joint research and development as well as joint production or both. However, the research and development must be significant where production is included. There are restrictions as to the size of the parties and their market share. Clearly, this may prevent the block exemption from applying to the majority of agreements where innovations are concerned as happened in KSB/Goulds/Lowara/IT. The extent of territorial protection permitted is narrow. Parties may allocate manufacturing territories and may agree to not actively solicit sales for 5 years after the goods are first put on the market, within the Common Market, in each other's territories. Any further protection is black listed. This is less than the protection given under the Patent Licensing Regulation.

4.7.5 CONCLUSION ON ARTICLE 85

In conclusion, therefore, the argument put forward is that Article 130r(2) does not offer undertakings a trump card against the application of Article 85 of the Treaty. Nevertheless, if an agreement can be shown to have environmentally beneficial effects, such affects, must be taken into account when considering the application of Article 85 to the agreement. Further, considerable weight should be given to such effects thereby improving the chances of either finding that the agreement does not restrict competition or that exemption should be granted under Article 85(3). The environmental record of an agreement adds to its quality and this alone should improve an agreement's chances of exemption if a restriction of competition is found within the meaning of Article 85(1). Provided that such benefits are passed on to the consumer (although the concept of consumer does not include the public at large benefitting from a cleaner environment), and that the restrictions included in the agreement are considered indispensable to achieving that aim, the agreement should be exempted under Article 85(3). With regard to block exemptions, a similar favourable approach should be taken either under the opposition procedure, or when considering the question of withdrawal of the benefit of an exemption. Further, if an agreement threatens to cause considerable harm to the environment, even though it complies with the provisions of a relevant block exemption the Commission should withdraw the benefit of automatic exemption.

4.7.6 ARTICLE 86: ABUSE OF A DOMINANT POSITION

The Council's Resolution of 3rd December 1992 concerns the relationship between industrial competitiveness and environmental protection. OJ [1992] C331/5. It states that the development and implementation of measures to protect and improve the environment should take into account the nature of the product to be addressed, the efficiency of measures and the potential benefits and costs of action or lack of action. It also states however, that all such measures 'which distort competition with the Community or restrict trade must ... be avoided in accordance with the provisions of the Treaty'. Those provisions include not only Article 85 but also Article 86.

Article 86 seeks the same aim as Article 85, namely the maintenance of effective or workable competition. Its scope of application differs from Article 85 in that it is aimed at individual action by undertakings which hold market power. Nevertheless, the distinction between the two Articles has been blurred slightly by the introduction of joint dominance by the Commission and the Court in Italian Flat Glass [1990] 4 CMLR 535.

4.7.6.1 SCOPE OF ARTICLE 86

Article 86 applies only to firms which have market power and which seek to use such power in an abusive manner. The Court has held the Article to be directly effective in the sense that it is enforceable before national Courts.

Unlike Article 85, Article 86 does not explicitly provide for exemptions. Nevertheless, the recent practice of the Commission has been to allow undertakings to provide justifications for the behaviour and, within the negotiation process, an informal exemption approach has been made. In essence, the Commission will balance the abusive practice against the benefits and justification put forward.

4.7.6.2 DOMINANT POSITION

The concept of a dominant position with EC Competition law is slightly different from the economists' concept of power over price. In Continental Can [1972] CMLR D11, the Commission explained that 'undertakings are in a dominant position when they have power to behave independently, which puts them in a position to act without taking into account their competitors, purchasers or suppliers. That is the position when, because of their share of the market, or of their share of the market combined with the availability of technical knowledge, raw materials or capital, they have the power to determine prices or to control production or distribution for a significant part of the products in question. This power does not necessarily have to derive from an absolute domination permitting the undertakings which hold it to eliminate all will on the part of their economic partners. It is sufficient that they be strong enough as a whole to ensure to those undertakings an overall independence of behaviour, even if there are differences in intensity in their influence on the different partial markets'. Although power over price is not essential, it will usually be found to accompany dominance.

In Continental Can, Case 6/72 Europemballage & Continental Can v Commission [1973] ECR 215, the Court insisted on the Commission analyzing a firm's market power in two steps; first, it should define the relevant market and then it should assess the firm's dominance on that market. The Commission has adopted this practice but has tended to define markets narrowly in the first stage and then to ignore that definition when assessing a firm's dominance. The approach is clearly a fluid one, and provided that all of the relevant factors are taking into account, exactly when they are included does not matter.

4.7.6.2.1 RELEVANT MARKET

The Commission defines the relevant market in terms of both demand side and supply side substitutes. Demand side substitutes relates to those products which take into account their physical characteristics, uses and price, are in the eyes of the consumer interchangeable. Supply side substitutability on the other hand, considers the market from the point of view of the manufacturer. The question asked is whether an undertaking producing one product could, without excessive time or costs, switch its production to the manufacturer of a different product.

The Court has insisted on the Commission undertaking an analysis of the supply side. Nevertheless, the Commission has tended to favour the demand side approach.

The narrower the definition of the market the greater the risk that a firm will be found dominant on it. Consequently, notwithstanding the environmental aspects of a product, firms would be advised to suggest to the Commission that the relevant market includes both ecologically friendly and unfriendly products. Unfortunately, as eco-industry develops this argument will be more difficult to sustain. At some point users will cease to consider the eco-friendly products as being equivalent in view of their characteristics, price and intended use to products which harm the environment. The eco record of a product is clearly one of its characteristics. As consumers come to prefer products with a low environmental impact they will at some point consider them as not being interchangeable with environmentally harmful products even if the two are physically identical.

In addition to the definition of the relevant product market, the Commission and Court will define the relevant geographical market. The geographic market is that in which the conditions of competition are alike for traders. Once those conditions change, regardless of the reason why, the geographic market border will be drawn. The geographic market may be local, regional, national or EC wide. Transport costs, barriers to entry and other factors will be taken into account. Consequently, in the present state of environmental legislation, differences in environmental standards required by national law may reduce markets for some eco-products to Member State borders. Nevertheless, as the harmonization of environmental standards continues within the internal market programme, so these borders will be dropped. On the other hand, it may be argued that because of the principle that environmental damage or pollution be rectified at source, so the drawing of markets for environmental products should be restricted to the local level. Although a case dealing with free trade rather than competition, the Court held in Case 2/90 Commission v Belgium, Walloon Import Ban Case, that waste produced in one area is in essence different from waste produced in another because of the application of the disposal at source principle. This justifies regional measures affecting the treatment of foreign waste from the way in which home produced waste was to be disposed of. Such a rule was not discriminatory because of the difference in the waste on account of the way it was produced. The application of this and other principles to environmental products as a whole may be an argument for the drawing of narrow geographical markets. Again, this may be to the disadvantage of companies operating in the eco-industry since their chances of being found dominant would be increased.

Markets are considered over a certain time scale. In Case 332/81 Michelin v Commission [1983] ECR 3461, the Court accepted that the Commission should assess the cross-elasticities of supply and demand over a certain time scale. However, the time scale adopted was shorter than would be used by economists. Economists suggest that competition operates in the long-term defined as the time needed to build new plant. The Court and Commission on the other hand considered a time scale of a matter of a few years at the maximum. In Michelin the Court observed that it takes time to build a factory, or for customers to assess the quality of a new brand or product. Consequently the creation of the capacity could be ignored. This approach overemphasised the market's position of the undertaking concerned and again is unfavourable to undertakings. It increased the likelihood of their being found dominant.

4.7.6.2.2 FACTORS AFFECTING DOMINANCE

Having defined the relevant markets a number of other factors are taken into account when assessing where a firm is dominant on that market.

The principal theatre of enquiry is the market share of the undertaking concerned. Whilst specific figures have not been suggested by the Court or Commission, it is highly likely that any firm with more than 40% of the market will be considered dominant unless specific factors can be shown to negate such a presumption: see Case 26/76 United Brands v Commission [1978] ECR 207. Anything less than 10% market share can be disregarded. Between those two figures, the Commission and Court will require convincing evidence that the undertaking concerned is subject to competition and has no market power.

This approach has serious consequences for undertakings attempting to introduce innovative technology. If the Commission considers that their market is restricted to the new product, the undertaking will be found clearly to have a dominant position. It will therefore have to be careful not to abuse its power. Nevertheless, where new technology is concerned, the Commission has taken a lenient approach on the grounds that the market is new. This is explained further below.

In addition to market share, the Commission will consider the financial backing enjoyed by the undertaking. The greater its financial resources, the more likely it is to be able to act independently of competitors and customers. Developments in the legal consequences of financial support provided by banks and other financial institutions to manufacturing companies may have an effect on the way in which dominance is defined for any given undertaking.

Taking the UK as an example, the effect of the Environmental Protection Act 1990 ("EPA") and the Water Act 1989 is to diminish the value of security held by financial institutions for money lent to undertakings. This will have an effect on the willingness of the financial sector to grant facilities if there are any environmental risks attendant upon the activities or premises of the proposed borrower. Similarly, banks and insolvency practitioners may face liabilities themselves particularly when becoming involved in the running of a business during its liquidation. Such liability may arise because the financial institution becomes the owner of the land or premises in question or becomes the occupier and so is liable for clean-up costs under the EPA for waste disposal and for trade effluence under the EPA Section 59 and the Water Industry Act 1991 Section 118 respectfully. Further, bankers and insolvency practitioners may become involved in participating in the running of the company or managing and thereby may well find themselves incurring liabilities under environmental law. The new generation of environmental statutes casts a wide net over candidates for environmental liability. It includes directors, managers, secretaries or other similar officers of the company or a person purporting to act in such capacity. Such persons may be liable, as well as their respective companies, when an offence is committed with their consent or connivance or has been attributed to the neglect of them (see EPA Section 157; Water Resources Act 1991 Section 217; Water Industry Act 1991 Section 210; Health & Safety at Work Act 1974 Section 37). The more a lender interferes with the general business of a company the more it is likely to be held liable under environmental law in respect of managerial decisions. This may occur in any of three ways. First, the lender may nominate directors to the Board; secondly, it may act in a similar way to a shadow director who, for the purposes of insolvency law, is treated as a normal director. Thirdly, the lender may have some control over the business if its employees participate in its running. This could be under the terms of a loan agreement.

The obligations on such bank or insolvency practitioners relate to pollution control, waste management, the depositing of waste, and the discharge of matter into controlled waters (territorial waters, coastal waters, inland fresh waters and ground waters).

Clearly, the scope of liability under environmental statue or common law (nuisance or negligence) of bankers, lenders or insolvency practitioners is great. This may have considerable repercussions on their willingness to lend to undertakings which do not have environmental policy or which operate on contaminated land, or which dispose of waste improperly. On the other hand, the more environmentally aware and proactive a company, the more likely it is to attract financial assistance. This may well have an effect on its ability to compete and therefore ultimately on its market power.

In conclusion on dominant position, therefore, it is not easy to advise what the relevant market may be in any given case. As suggested above, developments in demand for environmental product may result in the carving out of specific eco-markets. This will be to the disadvantage of environmentally friendly firms unless and until such markets become sufficiently deconcentrated as to allow free competition to operate. Similarly, another cause of concern is the short time scale over which the Court and Commission consider competitive forces. The shorter the time scale the less likely it is to argue before the Commission or Court that innovations will soon face other competition and therefore not confer on the innovator market power. Finally, the consequences of environmental liability for lenders may have an effect on the ability of undertakings without environmental policies to attract investment.

4.7.6.3 ABUSE

Having established that a given undertaking enjoys a position of dominance in its market, the Commission then investigates and characterises its market behaviour. The investigation is not limited to the market in which power is enjoyed, but also encompasses all other markets in which the firm is active. The market power in one market may be 'abused' by the dominant undertaking in other markets in which the company is not dominant.

An important question relating to the Commission's interpretation of Article 86 is whether the analysis under Article 85 is different from that under Article 86. Early applications of Articles 85 and 86 by both the Commission and Court focused on their different structures. Article 85 divides into two with the express possibility of exemption notwithstanding an initial finding that the agrement restricts competition. Article 86 applies a single test and so, it was thought, merited a different approach. In essence, once abuse was found no justification could be put forward.

More recent Commission decisions including AKZO OJ [1985] L374/1; Boosey and Hawkes OJ [1987] L286/36; Hilti OJ [1988] L65/19; British Sugar OJ [1988] L284/41; Tetrapak OJ [1988] L272/27; Sabena OJ [1988] L317/47; BPB Industries & British Gypsum OJ [1989] L10/50; and Magill TV Guide OJ [1989] L78/43, appear, however, to indicate that the different structures of the two Articles has little effect on the method and substantive analysis adopted.

Under Article 86, the Commission has first looked to see if there is any restrictive behaviour, similar to Article 85(1) analysis. Then it has investigated any foreclosure effect, similar to the last criterion in Article 85(1) (possibility to eliminate competition in a substantial part of the product concerned). Finally, it is concerned with a projective justification which will trump the restrictive effects - similar to the first three criteria in Article 85(3) (improvement of production or distribution; promotion of technical or economic progress; and consumers obtain a fare share of the benefit).

There are two main differences, however. Article 85(3) prevents exemption when undertakings achieve monopoly power. This is, after all, the most obvious situation when the undertakings concerned are 'afforded the possibility of eliminating competition in respect of a substantial part of the products in question. Article 86 does not proscribe the acquisition of monopoly power. Acquisition of power is a neutral element. The Article is only concerned with the consolidation or strengthening of such power.

The second difference is the chronology in which the various criteria are applied. Under Article 85(3) everything can be lost if the Commission finds that the foreclosure effect of the agreement, i.e., the possibility to eliminate competition, is significant notwithstanding the agreement satisfies all other criteria. In Article 86, there must be a finding of such foreclosure before the Commission can proceed.

As Luc Guyselen put it (Fordham Corporate Law Institute (1989), ed B Hawk, Chapter 27, para. 87):

"foreclosure appears to be Article 86's alpha whereas it is Article 85's omega."

This difference seems to suggest that a firm in a dominant position on its existing market will have a better chance of succeeding under Article 86 than it would under Article 85(3), since it retains the opportunity to test the restrictive effects of its behaviour.

In fact, the distinction is unlikely to make much difference. Foreclosure by an existing dominant firm, excluding competitors from the market, will be just as unjustifiable under Article 86 as it is barred under Article 85(3), however beneficial the conduct in other circumstances. Conversely, where the foreclosure effect is minor in comparison to the benefits, under Article 86 the behaviour will be just as easy to justify as it is eligible for exemption under Article 85(3).

Finally, the Commission is required to apply the principle of proportionality under both Articles. This means that the method chosen to achieve an otherwise legitimate object must be the least restrictive available. The principle is not expressly included in Article 86. Nevertheless, it has been applied consistently by the Commission and Court in their Article 86 decisions. Proportionality may cause problems. Firms will find it easier to establish a legitimate aim than to show that their behaviour is the least restrictive means of attaining it. In essence, it requires the proving of a negative.

Consequently, the method adopted by the Commission when applying Article 86 has begun to reflect that used under Article 85. This does not mean, however, that the content of the analysis is identical.

Article 86 gives an inexhaustive list of abusive conduct:

(a) directly or indirectly imposing unfair purchase or selling prices or other unfair trading conditions;

(b) limiting production, markets or technical development to the prejudice of consumers;

(c) apply dissimilar conditions to equivalent transactions with other trading parties, thereby placing them at a competitive disadvantage;

(d) making the conclusion of contracts subject to acceptance by the other parties of supplementary obligations which, by their nature or according to commercial usage, have no connection with the subject of such contracts.'

The first point to be made in regard to the definition of abuse is that such abuse must take place or have an effect within a substantial part of the Common Market. This requirement is similar to the 'effect on trade between Member States' jurisdictional criterion for the application of Article 85. It is not entirely clear how large an area amounts to a substantial part of the Common Market. Much depends upon the nature of the market concerned. In Cases 40 etc/73, Suiker Unie v Commission, Sugar, [1976] 1CMLR295, the Court stated that:

"... the pattern and volume of the production and consumption of the said product, as well as the habits and economic opportunities of ve"dors and purchasers must be considered."(para. 371).

Precedents are not of much assistance, therefore. An alternative interpretation of this requirement has been given by Advocate General Warner in BP v Commission Case 77/77 [1978] ECR 1513 in which he treated the qualification as a de minimis rule. He found that the fact that BP's customers in the Netherlands took less than 0.5% of the relevant spirits supplied in the Common Market did not prevent them from amounting to a substantial part of the Common Market. The criterion may constitute either a geographical division of or any other factor dividing customers. In nearly every case, however, the criterion will be satisfied if the Commission is dealing with a dominant firm.

The notion of 'abuse' or 'abusive exploitation' as it is defined in other language versions of the Treaty, is treated as an objective concept by the Court (see Case 85/76 Hoffman-la-Roche v Commission, Vitamins [1979] ECR 461). The examples in Article 86 itself can be divided into two groups: those types of behaviour which seek to exclude competitors from the market; and those which seek to exploit customers.

With regard to the first category, exclusionary conduct, the Commission's and Court's approach is similar to that found under

German law. Any attempt to exclude competitors by means other than the normal processes of competition constitutes abuse. The notion of normal methods of competition refers to the classic methods based on performance including price competition if not predatory, improvements in quality including research and development, and advertising. Exclusive dealing agreements or loyalty discounts on the other hand are not based on performance and may, therefore, constitute abuse.

The second type of abuse, exploitation, or unfair competition, is not concerned with the overall effect on the structure of the market. Its purpose is to ensure that the monopoly profit gained by the dominant firm is not reaped to the overall detriment of the market. Consequently, unfair prices, discriminatory treatment and refusals to deal on the grounds of nationality are impugned.

The main question of interest in this present study is the extent to which environmental issues are to be integrated into the definition and implementation of Article 86. The possibility of justifying behaviour that has foreclosure effects is a significant development. Benefits emanating from 'abuse' are not in themselves sufficient to justify the behaviour. Instead, the Commission and Court are concerned with the objective reasons for the abuse. The fact that benefits are reaped are secondary to the equation. In essence, the Commission will ask, for example, why high prices are charged for a given product. If a valid justification can be put forward by the dominant firm, the Commission may find the behaviour acceptable. The principle of proportionality - that the behaviour used is the least restrictive possible to achieve the legitimate aim - has an important role to play.

Article 130r(2) requires that the Commission treats environmental protection as a ground on which otherwise abusive conduct can be justified. As has been explained above, hoisting up the environmental protection petard is not in itself sufficient to justify abuse. First, the reason must be supported by empirical evidence. Secondly, the justification must pass the proportionality test. A number of hyperthetical situations follow to suggest how environmental protection may be used to justify particular types of abuse. Exclusionary conduct is considered first, followed by exploitation.

4.7.6.3.1 EXCLUSIONARY BEHAVIOUR

In Case 6/72, Europemballage & Continental Can v Commission [1973] ECR 215, the Court accepted the Commission's decision that Article 86 prohibits conduct that substantially reduces competition. In that case, a metal can manufacturer which enjoyed a dominant position purchased a competitor firm and thereby increased its market power. This was found to be an abuse under Article 86. In explaining this part of its judgment the Court stated:

"The provision is not only aimed at practices which may cause damage to consumers directly, but also at those which are detrimental to them through their impact on an effective competition structure, such as is mentioned in Article 3(f) EC. Abuse may therefore occur if an undertaking in a dominant position strengthens such position in such a way that the degree of dominance reached considerably fetters competition, ie. that only undertakings remain in the market whose behaviour depends on the dominant one." (Para. 26)

Although acquisition of market power by way of merger now falls within the scope of the Merger Regulation, 4064/89, the reasoning in Continental Can still applies. Most notably, in Case T-51/89, Tetrapak Rausing v Commission [1991] 4 CMLR 334, the Court of First Instance found that the acquisition of competing technology by a firm with a dominant position constituted abuse. The Court stressed the need to consider the acquisition of competitor technology within the circumstances obtaining, and in particular the effects of the acquisition on the structure of competition in the relevant market. The acquisition of the competing technology itself was not an abuse. The additional ingredient was a finding that the acquisition has an anti-competitive effect. In that case, the Commission had found that the acquisition of the technology 'strengthened Tetra's very considerable dominance but also had the effect of preventing, or at the very least considerably delaying, the entry of a new competitor into a market where very little if any competition is found'. This finding branded the acquisition as an abuse which was therefore prohibited under Article 86.

This approach will apply mutatis mutandis to 'eco-technology'. A firm with a dominant position which requires competing eco-technology will, if the effect is to reduce competition on the relevant market, will constitute abuse and be prohibited. The acquisition will therefore have to be undone. Such an approach should in most circumstances lead to the protection of the environment. The Commission's concern is that new technology is promoted and widely disseminated. Preventing one firm from controlling all sources of technology in a given market whether environmentally friendly or not, conforms to the Commission's approach. The more widely environmentally friendly technology is available, the more likely it is to be translated into products and services. Further, competition in eco-products will increase such that their prices will reduce and the range of consumer choice increase.

An alternative scenario will be where a firm which is dominant in a market, and which controls environmentally friendly technology, seeks to acquire competing non eco-technology. Its justification may be on the ground of Article 130 r(2) that it is attempting to eliminate environmentally harmful products from the market. The Commission should implement its environmental policy by condoning the acquisition. As explained above, as Community law stands at present environmental policy will not trump competition policy. The Commission will therefore consider whether competition on the market has been reduced to such an extent that workable competition no longer exists. If such is the case the environmental justification will be dismissed. The firm with market power will have to compete on the basis of the performance of its products and not by buying out the competition. On the other hand, where the dominant firm can show that competition will continue to exist because of he possibility of other strains of environmentally friendly technology being developed and entering the market through other independent undertakings, the acquisition may be accepted. A progressive approach to Article 130r(2) within the competition context will support such a decision.

In several cases, the Court has condemned systematic discrimination through the use of discount systems or rebates when the effect is to make competition by smaller competitors more difficult. Such behaviour is considered discriminatory and, when ad hoc, unfair or where systematic, anti-competitive.

The reasoning behind these decisions is that systematic discrimination forecloses the market to smaller firms and makes it harder for them to compete on their merits. Buyers which are given a small discount if they purchase from the dominant firm rather than from competitors of the dominant firm will be able to pass that discount onto its customers and thereby improve its position. That buyer will be foreclosed to other competitors and may be able to enhance its position on its own market.

Where such discounts can be shown to be based on actual savings by the dominant firm, they are acceptable. The discount relates to the performance of the dominant firm, and is therefore the product of active competition. On the other hand, where there is no such justification, such discounts are impugned. The argument that an environmentally friendly product should not be considered substitutable for its environmentally harmful counterpart has been suggested above. Once demand reflects this approach, a justification may be put forward on the basis that the discounts are not discriminatory. As the situation stands at present, however, such an argument is unlikely to be acceptable.

Another type of exclusionary behaviour which is condemned by the Commission under Article 86 is known as predatory pricing. The definition of predatory pricing under EC law has not yet been settled. Clearly where a dominant firm sells below cost in order to deter entry to its market, the notion of predatory pricing will be fulfilled. It is less clear whether predation includes charging particularly low prices, notwithstanding they are above cost, solely for the reason of deterring a potential entrant.

In AKZO OJ [1985] L374/22 the Commission and on appeal the Court in Case 62/86 condemned predatory pricing largely because of the intention to deter smaller firms entering the market. The actual analysis of prices against cost did not seem to be pivotal.

Whilst short-term discounts may be given for new products or technology, these must not last for more than an introductory period. Consequently, notwithstanding the environmentally friendly nature of a product, a firm with market power cannot sell it at a price which may be considered predatory merely on the basis that this will assist its introduction and consolidation on the market. Again, the competition policy will trump the environmental protection card.

One final method of exclusionary behaviour that has been condemned under Article 86 is tying. The paradigm is where a dominant firm refuses to supply goods or services over which it has a dominant position to those wishing to use them unless the buyer purchases a second product. The reason for tying may be to extend the dominant firm's market power from one product to another; alternatively it may be an attempt to increase the price of the second product above that which it would normally command.

The Court has condemned tying in Case 311/84 Telemarketing [1985] ECR 3261. A Company, CLT, stopped accepting spot advertisements that indicated a telephone number to be used by the public to obtain further information, unless the number given for Belgium was that of its own subsidiary. The Court ruled that:

"An abuse within the meaning of Article 86 is committed where, without any objective necessity, an undertaking holding a dominant position in a particular market reserves to itself or to an undertaking belonging to the same group an ancillary activity which might be carried out by another undertaking as part of its activities on a neighbouring but separate market, with the possibility of eliminating all competition from such undertakings."

The key to this analysis, therefore, is whether there is some objective necessity for the tie. This may be a technological necessity, for example, where a given product cannot function properly without the second product, or for safety reasons, for example, where a given product cannot operate safely without the second product. It is submitted that environmental protection requirements should be accepted as a justification for tying. For example, a company producing goods made of a particular plastic may require the purchaser to dispose of the product through the seller's subsidiary disposal company which has got particular facilities for recycling the given type of plastic. The test, however, is a stiff one. There must be an objective necessity for the tie. Article 130 r(2) suggests that the need to protect the environment should constitute such an objective reason. Each case will turn on its own facts. The argument is there for the taking.

4.7.6.3.2 UNFAIR COMPETITION

The second type of abuse is where a firm with market power seeks to exploit its customers.

The paradigm is unfair pricing. In Case 26/75 General Motors Continental v Commission [1975] ECR 1367, the Court confirmed in principle that it is an abuse to charge prices that are excessive in relation to the 'economic value' of a service or product. This has been confirmed in subsequent cases included Case 27/76 United Brands v Commission [1978] ECR 207 in which the Court stated:

"The imposition by an undertaking in a dominant position directly or indirectly of unfair purchase or selling prices is an abuse to which exception can be taken under Article 86 of the Treaty." (Paras. 248 and 249)

It is advisable therefore to ascertain whether the dominant undertaking has made use of the opportunities arising out of its dominant position in such a way as to reap trading benefits which it would not have reaped if there had been normal and sufficiently effective competition.

The key to the application of environmental protection requirements to the assessment of whether prices are unfair is the notion of 'economic value' of a given product. Environmental protection measures often lead to higher production costs. If a dominant firm voluntarily chooses to make its products and processes more environmentally friendly, this may result in an increase in the cost of its goods. It is submitted that such an increase should not be considered as being 'unfair'. As is explained above, the environmental record of a product is part of its quality and therefore part of its economic value. As such, provided that there is a definite link between the increased price and the environmental costs of production, there can be no abuse.

The imposition of other terms, either on the purchase or sale of goods by a dominant firm, has also been branded as abuse. The seminal case on refusals to supply is Case 6 & 7/73 Commercial Solvents v Commission [1974] ECR 223. Here the Court upheld the Commission's decision that Commercial Solvents, the only producer in the world on an industrial scale of raw materials from which the drug Ethambutol could be made, enjoyed a dominant position in the Common Market. The Court confirmed that it was abusive to refuse to supply the raw material to a customer which was on of the only three makers of the drug in the Common Market. The Advocate General Warner, treated the refusal to supply as an extreme example of discrimination. However he thought that there might in certain circumstances be a justification for not supplying a product over with a firm is dominant. One suggestion he put forward, was that it might be lawful never to supply a new product but to manufacture the derivative product oneself from the beginning. Such a justification would be in line with the approach to intellectual property rights.

On the facts of Commercial Solvents, the effect of the refusal to supply the customer was severe. Commercial solvents was the only maker of the raw material in the world. The purchaser was one of only three makers of the derivative in the Common Market. If it could not obtain supplies directly from Commercial Solvents its competitive position in an already concentrated market would be severely jeopardised.

It is submitted that one justification which should be accepted on the basis of Article 130 (2) is where the refusal to supply or to purchase is based on environmental grounds. An example might be where a dominant firm wishes to improve its environmental performance. It may decide only to purchase from undertakings which themselves have a positive ecological record. Alternatively it may choose to supply only to dealers or customers which have proven environmental policies. This change in the dominant firm's buying or selling practice may, by analogy with Commercial Solvents, constitute an abuse. It is submitted, however, that the requirements of environmental protection may in themselves constitute a justification for the refusal to supply to purchase in this context. Again, reliance may be made on the argument that the environmental record of a product adds to its quality. Environmentally friendly products are better and of a higher quality than products which harm the environment. Such behaviour, therefore, should not be branded as abusive.

4.7.6.3.3 ENVIRONMENTALLY HARMFUL BEHAVIOUR AS ABUSE

The list of abusive behaviour is not closed. Where a firm undertakes behaviour which is environmentally harmful to the exclusion of alternative environmentally friendly activity, it is submitted that if this has an effect on the competitive structure of the market concerned, there is an abuse under Article 86. In such a scenario it may be relatively easy to establish the anti-competitive effect. This may consist in the foreclosure to the market of the environmentally friendly technology or product; the erection of barriers to entry preventing environmentally friendly potential competition from entering the market; and, stifling new strains of environmentally friendly technology. Just as any behaviour which has the effect of separating the market is treated almost as an abuse per se, so, it is submitted environmentally harmful behaviour should be treated as an almost automatic abuse. This should be so whether it is combined with otherwise pro-competitive behaviour or not.

4.7.7 CONCLUSIONS ON ARTICLE 86

The fact that a firm with market power has a good ecological record is not, by itself, reason to disapply the competition rules to its activities. This is not required by Article 130 r (2) and would, in any case, infringe the competition policy of the Community.

On the other hand, the protection of the environment may be put forward as a justification for behaviour which would otherwise be classified as abusive. The Commission and Court have approached Article 86 in recent years in much the same way as they have treated Article 85. After finding foreclosure affects resulting form a dominant firm's anti-competitive behaviour, the institutions will listen to justifications for such behaviour. The justification cannot comprise only benefits resulting from the behaviour. It must put forward a legitimate aim for which the otherwise abusive behaviour is necessary. It is submitted that the protection of the environment must be taken as a legitimate aim which can justify otherwise abusive behaviour. An example may include higher prices for ecological products where the increase in price is reflected in the environmental costs, (in VOTOB, the Commission accepted that firms may pass on the cost of the polluter pays principle to customers). Another example would be purchasing only from undertakings which have a good ecological record.

4.8 MERGERS - THE MERGER REGULATION

Control of mergers has only recently become a specific element in the arsenal of the Commission;s competition law armoury. In a study published by the Commission in 1966 the Commission concluded that Article 85 did not apply to mergers, and that Article 86 did so only if one of the undertakings concerned was dominant and that the transaction constituted abuse, (see Commission Memorandum on Problem of Industrial Concentration in the Common Market, Competition Series No 3 (1966) ['the 1966 Memorandum']). Originally there was little concern over this lacuna in anti-trust control at the EC level because, like the coal and steel industries, mergers were encouraged in order to assist national integration in the Common Market. In the late 1960's, however, concentration studies by the Commission revealed that mergers tended to be national, (see Commission 1st Report on Competition Policy (1971), para. 205 and subsequent Reports on Competition Policy). This led the Commission to propose to the Council of Ministers in 1973 a regulation to control mergers from the competition policy point of view, (see Commission, 3rd Report on Competition Policy (1973) para. 28). Despite general favour, the Council was divided over the jurisdiction and scope of the proposal. Differences were only settled in the late 1980's with a degree of give and take on all sides, and spurred on by the Court of Justice's apparent endorsement of the Commission's use of Article 85 in merger type transactions in Cases 142 and 156/84 BAT v Commission (Phillip Morris) [1988] 4 CMLR 24. The most wide ranging concession by the Commission was wholesale disapplication of the implementing Regulation issued under Article 87, including Regulation 17/62, from all concentration transactions, whatever their size (see Article 22 (2) MR). Residual application of Articles 85 and 86 remains through Articles 88 and 89 of the EC Treaty by the commission and national authorities, but in the absence of investigative, sanctioning and discovery powers, this is likely to prove ineffective.

4.8.1 THE STRUCTURE OF THE MERGER REGULATION

Although all concentrations fall generally outside Articles 85 and 86, therefore, only those concentrations which have a 'community dimension' may be prohibited under the Merger Regulation, 4064/89 (Article 1 MR). The Community dimension test is a size of parties, rather than a size of transaction test. It is calculated upon the annual turnover of the parties to the transaction, including connected undertakings (i.e., parent, sister and daughter companies), in all of their global activities for the preceding financial year to the date of the transaction. There are special rules relating to the assessment of turnover (a) where only a part of an undertaking is acquired by another undertaking, and (b) when the concentration is between credit institutions, or insurance companies, (Article 5 MR). At present, the levels are the combined worldwide annual turnover for the financial year preceding the transaction of more than 5 billion ECU; at least two of the parties must have a community wide annual turnover of more than 250 million ECU for the same year; and all the parties must not have generated more than two-thirds of their community wide turnover in the same Member State.

The MR is directed at 'concentration' transactions. Concentrations are defined in Article 3(1) MR as arising when (a) two or more undertakings merge or (b) one or more persons already controlling at least on undertaking, acquire direct or indirect control of the whole or parts of at least one other undertaking. Consequently, the scope of the MR is much broader than the general understanding of a merger. Acquisition by one undertaking of part of another may constitute a merger, as may the joint acquisition or formation of an undertaking by two independent companies - a concentrative joint venture. It should be noted, however, that the Commission draws a distinction between joint ventures which fall within the MR in which the parent companies are neither actual nor potential competitors of each other nor of the joint ventures which fall within the scope of Article 85 and of which the parties are either actual or potential competitors. Further, a joint venture must be an independent entity capable of operating on a market through its own resources and personnel, and without a due reliance upon its parents.

Concentrations with Community dimension are by Article 2 MR to be declared as incompatible with the Common Market if they create or strengthen a dominant position as a result of which effective competition would be significantly impeded. 'Dominant position' is not defined by the MR. Not surprisingly, therefore, the Commission has drawn on its own understanding and that of the Court of Justice of the concept under Article 86, and in particular cases, such as Case 885/76 Hoffman-la-Roche v Commission (Vitamins) [1979] 2 CMLR 211 and Case 322/81 Michelin v Commission [1985] 1 CMLR 282. In essence, the test is not the same as power over price, which is the test found in some economists' literature, but rather the ability to influence the market by the undertaking's own conduct, neither hindered by competitors, nor by the existence of other markets' participants' dependence for survival on the dominant enterprise, nor by the economic and financial power which gives the dominant enterprise advantages in any competitive battle. As under Article 86, the definition of dominance is preconditioned by assessing the relevant product, geographic and temporal markets. The analysis is much the same as under Article 86 - using demand side substitutability together with supply side substitutability over a relative short time period.

It should be noted, however, that the Commission's approach to dominance under the MR is slightly different from that under Article 86, in that the thresholds appear to be lower. Whereas under Article 86 the Court of Justice has considered that there is a presumption of dominance when an undertaking has 40% or more market share, under the MR in recital 14 lowers the market share at which the presumption operates at 25%.

The MR applies to both the creation and strengthening of a dominant position. The former occurs when, through a merger or by the creation of a concentrative joint venture, the parent company acquires the necessary levels of market power to be dominant. Strengthening of a dominant position is no more than a consolidation by either increasing an undertaking's economic or financial backing, or by increasing its market share to the detriment of other competitors.

4.8.2 THE MERGER REGULATION AND ENVIRONMENTAL PROTECTION

The crucial question for this present study is the extent to which ecological considerations can be taken into account when assessing whether a merger creates or strengthens a dominant position in the Common Market as a result of significantly impeding effective competition. The test for incompatibility of a merger is different from that under Article 85 where instead of the need to find significant impediment of effective competition, under Article 85 it is sufficient for there to be no more than a restriction of competition. The basic test in Article 2 MR appears to be solely competition policy based. However, Article 2 MR includes a number of other criteria which should be taken into account. Article 2(1)(b) MR refers to the development of technical and economic progress. Concentrations which cannot be condoned on competition grounds may be defended if such progress is sufficiently important. It should be noted that the industrial progress defence is limited and that any development must be to the advantage of consumers, and must not form an obstacle to competition. The timescale over which consumer advantages are to be realised is not disclosed and will probably depend on the industry concerned. It should be remembered that the Commission favours the short term. Further, any obstacle to competition is sufficient to defeat the defence. This means that to be effective, the technical or economic progress concerned must not be associated with any restriction on competition, apart from those already inherent in the merger itself. Any technical or economic progress which entrenches firms in dominant market positions and enables the undertakings to reduce output and raise price will not be to consumer advantage and is unlikely to pass muster with the Commission. Further, if some less restrictive means of achieving the same results is available without undue cost, the defence is unlikely to succeed.

Despite these restrictions on the defence, there is clearly an argument as has been explained above, that improvements in environmental protection as a result of new products should be considered under the rubric of economic and technical progress. The ecological record of a product adds to its quality. If new technology is developed to improve the ecological record, therefore, necessary progress can be shown to have been made, which in turn will lead to a better economic situation overall.

Nevertheless, the limitations to the defence should not be underestimated. It is likely that an industrial policy defence may well be available only when there is still doubt over the creation or strengthening of a dominant position after all the other criteria in Article 2 MR have been examined.

It may be significant that the industrial policy defence is the last mentioned of the factors listed in Article 2(1) MR. The most obvious case would be of a concentration between undertakings with operations in a variety of markets in which technology is important - for example, eco-industry. Reference to the technological effects of the merger, including its environmental benefits, might help to convince the Commission that in markets which are resilient to dominance (such as those in which competition in technology is strong) the concentration is benign. Further, it should be noted that the Commission may use its case law under Article 85 EC to assist its deliberations under the MR. This may help Counsel to construct defence arguments in particular cases. The burden of proving industrial progress, including environmental protection benefits, lies on the parties concerned.

The 13th Recital to the MR expressly refers to Articles 2 and 130a

EC . The criteria mentioned in these Articles includes social and economic cohesion, harmonious development and new improvement in the standards of living. In contrast to the industrial policy defence, these criteria are not expressly disapplied if an obstacle to competition results. Thus they may well carry more weight than the industrial policy defence. The reference to the improvement in the standard of living is clearly the key by which environmental concerns can be integrated into merger decisions. Further, this is, of course, required by Article 130r(2).

The principle of proportionality is likely to inform the Commission's approach to defence based on the environmental record of a given product or process arising out of the merger. Any merger which strengthens an undertaking's ability and opportunity to reduce output and raise prices is unlikely to be defended successfully by any non-competition based argument. The same approach is discussed under Article 85 and 86 applies to the MR. Article 130r(2) EC and the 13th Recital to the MR do not provide for an exemption from the MR if the concentration is beneficial for the environment though it does require that the Regulation is interpreted in an ecologically sound manner.

Article 2(1)(a) MR refers to the need to take into account 'the structure of all the markets concerned within ... the Common Market' (emphasis added). This suggests that beneficial effects on different markets from that on which the concentration concerned is consummated may be used in the defence of the merger. This may provide the vehicle for arguments that a merger between two undertakings with the aim of improving environmental protection in other markets should be approved notwithstanding some harm caused to the market on which the undertakings are active. An example might be where undertakings in the energy industry merge to improve the possibility of environmentally friendly methods of energy creation and/or conservation, with considerable effects on the environmental consequences of other markets.

Unfortunately, the omens from the Commission for the use of non-competition based defences in Article 2 are unfavourable. In its Aerospatiale-Aliena De Haviland, Case IV/MO53, OJ [1991] L334/42, the Commission stated categorically that it was determined to use the MR as an economic tool to competition ends only. The then Commissioner for Competition Policy, Sir Leon Brittan, has stated publicly that industrial policy, borrowed from Article 85(3) EC and in Article 2 MR shall not be read as justifying trade-offs between competition and other economic objectives:

"In a competitive market, mergers may or may not give rise to technical and economic progress. In an uncompetitive market, even if they do, they will not be allowed."

It should be remembered, however, that the De Haveland decision was made prior to the amendments to the EC Treaty by the TEU. Although the existing Article 130r(2) was drafted in a similar vein to the amendment by the TEU, as explained above, the emphasis on integration of environmental policy has been strengthened since the amendment. This may suggest that a different approach should be taken by the Commission in its future decisions under the MR.

As regards procedure, all concentrations which have a Community dimension must be notified to the Commission under the special notification procedure set down by the MR and its Implementing Regulation, Regulation 2356/90 (IR). The merger must be suspended until the Commission comes to a decision. The Commission's investigatory process is in two stages. Within one month of notification, the Commission must come to a preliminary view that either the concentration is acceptable or that a further investigation is necessary. If the Commission finds the concentration acceptable, it must publish a decision to that effect and the merger may go ahead. If on the other hand a further investigation is necessary, the Commission will notify the parties and will embark upon a four month more detailed investigation of the merger and its effects. At the end of the investigation, the Commission must come to a decision of either approval or disapproval. If the merger is approved, it may be implemented. If disapproved, it must not go ahead. Failure by the Commission to abide by the time limits results in a decision of compatibility of the concentration.

4.8.3 CONCLUSION ON THE APPLICATION OF THE MERGER REGULATION

The effects of the application of Article 130r(2) EC on the MR are that just as in all other Community measures, environmental consideration must now be respected. Consequently, the Commission can only approve the concentration if it does not hamper the environment significantly. In essence, therefore, there is an additional requirement over and above the competition based criteria set down in Article 2 MR. However, because environmental protection is not itself the prevailing goal, mergers cannot be defended purely on the basis of ecological considerations. They must still satisfy the competition policy as defined in the MR. Nevertheless, the Commission must take a conscious decision whenever approving or disapproving a merger that there are no risks of serious environmental damage consequential upon the proposed merger. It may be arguable as the need for sustainable development grows, that in the future, environmental protection will become the prevailing goal. If so, the competition and environmental aspects of any given concentration must be balanced. Priority should be given to environmental concerns.

4.9 STATE INTERVENTION AND COMPETITION

Until the introduction of the Fifth Environmental Action Programme by the Commission, the majority of the Community's work to protect the environment focused on the enactment of legislation. The activities in Brussels have been reflected to a limited extent by national legislation. The question posed here is the extent to which agreements encouraged by State authorities, which on the one hand restrict competition but on the other hand are designed to protect the environment, are subject to Articles 85 and 86.

The Community's approach is two-fold. First, under Article 5 EC, Member States are obliged not to render the competition rules ineffective. Consequently, should a Member State enact measures which require restrictive agreements to be entered by undertakings, the Member State has breached obligations within the Treaty, and is exposed to an action by the Commission under Article 169 of the Treaty. The policy was set out by the Court in Case 229/83 Leclerc v Au Ble Vert [1985] ECR 1:

"Whilst it is true that the rules on competition are concerned with the conduct of undertakings and not with the national legislation, Member States are nonetheless obliged under the second paragraph of Article 5 of the Treaty not to detract, by means of national legislation, from the full and uniform application of Community law or from the effectiveness of its implementing measures; nor may they introduce or maintain in force measures, even of a legislative nature, which may render ineffective the competition rules applicable to undertakings."

(Para. 11).

The same approach should be taken towards State measures which are designed deliberately to harm the environment even if they are intended to encourage competition.

The second prong of the Community's approach is the application of Article 85 to agreements notwithstanding their encouragement by national measures. In Case 123/83 BNIC v Clair [1985] ECR 392, the Court stated that Government encouragement or persuasion is no defence to Article 85. In that case, the recommendation by a private trade association of minimum prices for cognac infringed Article 85 although the Association was set up at the request of the relevant Minister who appointed the Chairman and sent a Nominee to its meetings. Further, the recommendation was not excused by a subsequent ministerial order that made the prices binding on non-members.

Further, State Members which reinforce the effects of anti-competitive agreements do not protect the agreements from violating Article 85. In Case 311/85 Vlaamse Reisbureaus v Commission, Belgium Travel Agents [1989] 4 CMLR 213, the Court ruled that the professional rules of conduct that forbade price competition within the travel agency industry should not be applied to undertakings within the industry when the original agreement within the professional had expired but that the rules themselves had been maintained by Royal decree.

Where State Members oblige anti-competitive activity by undertakings, the latter have a defence to the application of Article 85. Nevertheless, the Commission will investigate thoroughly whether there was nay means of avoidance of the national rules. The State measure will however, be invalid for infringing the competition rules.

The application of these principles to the area of environmental protection suggests that national measures requiring undertakings to enter into agreements for the protection of the environment must not infringe the competition rules. Nevertheless, should they do so, the activities of the undertakings concerned will not expose the latter to fines under competition rules. The undertakings must, however, immediately cease compliance with the national measure and competition should be restored. This approach should be applied to the converse situation. Article 130 r (2) must require Member States to take into account the requirements of the protection of the environment as set out within Article 130 R (1) when applying their competition rules. The encouragement of activity which threatens considerable harm to the environment will be no defence to the suggested application of Article 85 above if competition is at the same time effected.

4.10STATE AIDS

4.10.1STATE AIDS, ENVIRONMENTAL PROTECTION AND EC LAW

Within the EC system aids are governed by Articles 92 and 93 EC. The purpose of these Articles is to prevent government behaviour creating distortions of competition in the market place and between the states themselves. The rules form part of the competition policy. The main criticism raised by the Commission is that state aids favour national producers and 'transfer difficulties onto other competitors in other states' (see 12th Commission Report on Competition 1983 para.158).

State aids may be granted for a variety of reasons. They may be used to ward off the short term effects of recession; to invest in plant or innovations where private institutions are reluctant; to restrict industry; to assist privatisation programmes; to encourage the development of environmental friendly technologies; and to ward off the effects of the polluter pays principle.

It is important to note that Article 92 does not follow the same format as Article 85. Significantly, state aid may be granted in certain circumstances. Article 92 sets out very flexible definitions of categories of aid that are either ipso facto valid (Article 92 (2)) or potentially valid (Article 92(3)).

Article 130r(2) requires that when assessing the validity of state aid, the Commission must take into account the environmental consequences. It is submitted that where state aid is used to subvert the principles set out in the environmental policy of the Community such state aid should be prohibited. On the other hand, where state aid is used to facilitate the introduction of environmental technology a favourable attitude should be given.

4.10.2DEFINITION OF STATE AID

The definition of state aid is broad. A number of discreet elements must be satisfied:

(a) the aid must be granted by a member state or through state resources;

(b) the aid can take form whatsoever;

(c) the aid must distort or threaten to distort competition by favouring certain undertakings for the production of certain goods; and

(d) the aid must affect trade between member states.

The Court held in Case 30/59 Steenkolenmijnen v High Authority [1971] ECR 1, that aid is wider than a mere subsidy:

"The concept of an aid is ... wider than that of a subsidy because it embraces not only positive benefits, such as subsidies themselves, but also interventions which, in various forms, mitigate the charges which are normally included in the budget of an undertaking and which would without, there being subsidies in the strict sense of the word be similar in character and have the same effect."

The variety of forms in which aid may be granted appears to be infinite. Examples can be found in the Annual Competition Reports of the Commission. They include low interest rate loans, sales to undertakings at an undervalue, injections of capital, direct cash handouts, investment by the state in the equity of an undertaking, payment of bonuses and so on.

Aid must contain an element of gratuity. This means therefore that if consideration or count of any benefit is given by the undertaking concerned to the state or to some third party, there can be no aid within the meaning of Article 92. It should be noted, however, that the existence of some gratuity is not pivotal. What is necessary is that some benefit is given when in the normal circumstances of the market it would not be available. An example would be where a state grants a loan to an undertaking in circumstances when independent investors would not be attracted to do so.

The aid must be granted by the Member State or through the member states' resources. Consequently aid may be granted by central or local government or any other public or private agency subject to control by the State. The State's involvement may be direct or indirect. In Case 290/83 Commission v France [1985] ECR 439, a payment made by the Caisse Nationale de Credit Agricole (a public body) out of surplus proceeds of private funds was held to be state aid because the payment was initiated by the State. Consequently, it is not necessary that the benefit should come out of the governmental revenue.

The great width of state aid comes from the notion that it can take any form whatsoever. Any measure, apart from general measures, which has the effect of reducing the costs otherwise placed on an undertaking in relation to its commercial activity, and which therefore affects the structure of competition on the relevant market, is aid. Clearly, any individual measure (as opposed to a general measure) which has the effect of diverting the costs of pollution away from the polluter should constitute aid. This may be by assistance in dispersing clean up costs or reductions in the tax on undertakings which pollute should they carry out clean up themselves. Alternatively, it may be through grants to companies to encourage them to undertake research and development into environmentally friendly technology. The list of possible examples is endless.

The aid must distort or threaten to distort competition by favouring certain undertakings or the protection of certain goods. It is assumed that the same principles which have been developed under Article 85 are applied to state aid. Again a distinction is drawn between individual measures and general measures. The latter are exempt.

Finally, the aid must affect trade between member states. The same interpretation as under Articles 85 and 86 applies to Article 92.

4.10.3 AID THAT IS AUTOMATICALLY COMPATIBLE: ARTICLE 92(2)

Although such aid as is specified in Article 92(2) is automatically valid, it is still subject to supervision by the Commission. Such supervision is designed to ensure that the aid does fall within the permitted categories.

The first category of such aid is that to individual consumers of a non-discriminatory nature insofar as the origin of goods is concerned. An example put forward by Advocate General Reischl in Case 52/76 Benedetti v Munari [1977] ECR 163, is where the state acquires wheat at the intervention price and resells it at a discount having the effect of reducing bread prices. In essence, the consumers, the people who buy bread, gain aid through the artificial non-market prices.

The second example concerns aid to ameliorate the consequences of natural disasters or exceptional circumstances. Clearly within this category would come aid to assist in the clean up of environmental disasters such as Chernobyl, 'The Braer', Bhopal and so on.

4.10.4 STATE AID THAT MAY BE COMPATIBLE: ARTICLE 92(3)

Categories of aid covered by Article 92(3) may be compatible with the Common Market but to do so it requires a formal Commission clearance decision.

The Article itemises four categories of aid, three of which are subject to Commission decision, and one of which is subject to the Council.

The three categories of aid subject to Commission decision are:

(a) Regional aid,

(b) Aid to promote projects of Common, European interest, or to remedy a serious disturbance in the economy of a member state; and

(c) Sectoral aid which does not diversely effect trading conditions to an unacceptable degree.

Two of these categories of aid, that used to promote projects of common European interest, and that described as sectoral aid which does not adversely affect trade conditions to an unacceptable degree, may be used as basis for clearing state assistance given to environmental projects.

The Court accepted the Commission's criteria used when deciding whether to approve aid in Case 730/79 Phillip Morris v Commission [1980] ECR 2671:

(a) the aid must promote or further a project that is in the Community's interest as a whole; aid which promotes national interest is unacceptable;

(b) the aid must be necessary for the achievement of the result in (a);

(c) the aid must be proportional to the importance of the legitimate aim. Consequently, the Commission will consider the duration, intensity and ambit of the aid and the anti-competitive risks associated with it.

(d) Finally, the principle of proportionality is applied in the sense that the Commission and Court must be satisfied that the beneficiaries could not have attained the objective in question without the aid. This is similar to the criterion of indispensability in Article 85(3).'

The first category of areas covered by Article 92(3) which may have relevance for environmental policy is that of aid to promote the execution of an important project of common European interests. The Commission has already permitted aid to encourage energy saving projects and environmental schemes. Details of these can be found in the annual reports on competition policy of the Commission.

The second category is that of sectoral and regional aid. This may be granted to facilitate the development of certain economic activities (sectoral aid). The Commission's policy was laid down in it Communication to the Council of May 1978. This laid down policy guidelines in respect of aid for investment or for crisis or rescue measures. Sectoral aid is to be considered as the exception to the rule and justified only where:

(1) there was real need;

(2) the aid would lead to the restoration of long-term liability;

(3) the aid would make a positive contribution to the economic, social and regional policies for the Community;

(4) the aid was intended to bring about adjustments to changing economic structures and not to preserving industrial sectors unchanged despite economic development; and

(5) the aid will be proportional to the object sought to be achieved.

These polices were confirmed in 1987 in the 17th Report on Competition Policy where the Commission stated:

"As far as possible aids should be depressive, if granted over time, and should not deviate more than absolutely necessary for the basis principle of undistorted competition in the Community. The granting of state aids by one Member State must not lead to the transfer of industrial difficulties and unemployment to other Member States, nor should inefficient companies be artificially kept in existence through state aid to the detriment of their efficient competitors in other member states. This aspect must be reemphasised in the perspectives of 1992, as undertakings will only adjust their activities, optimise their resource allocation and bring to the Community the benefits of the Single Market if they can be reasonably certain of gaining the just benefits from such action and do not face unfair competition from rivals receiving state aid." (Para.206)

This suggests that aid granted to assist environmental development must first of all be depressive. It may be granted to encourage initiatives but cannot be used as a prop for long term developments. It is submitted, however, that a more favourable attitude should be given to environmental aid rather than to other types of aid. Again, it should be remembered that the quality of a product can be improved by its ecological record. This in turn amounts to economic benefit and eventually, if the aid is truly depressive, competition on the relevant markets should be increased.

Further, it is argued that eco-industry should be considered as a separate sector alongside those sectors already covered by state aid, such as synthetic fibres; ship building; automobiles and steel for example.

Aid which is granted to overcome the environmental consequences of industrial activity should, it is submitted, as a result of Article 130r(2), be carefully scrutinised by the Commission. If the purpose is to maintain an industry which is environmentally harmful, it is submitted that this runs contrary to the Commission's policy set out in the 17th Report on Competition Policy. In particular the aid should be characterised as preserving industrial sectors unchanged despite economic developments. Such developments should, it is submitted, include environmental changes which will have an effect on the economic structure of the Community,

4.10.5 PROCEDURE AND SUPERVISION OF STATE AIDS

The rules governing the procedure and supervision of the state aid is set out in Article 93. The institution with responsibility for the implementation of Articles 92 and 93 is the Commission. The rules are different depending upon whether the aid is existing aid or new aid. Article 93(2) is directed at existed aid. Article 93(1) places an obligation on the Commission and the Member States to keep all systems of aid in constant review. Should the Commission consider that measures are necessary it must propose appropriate steps to Member States concerned in relation to any particular aid. Once such a proposal is given, Article 93(2) procedure may be started. The opening stance, therefore, for Article 93(2) is that the aid concerned is prima facie incompatible with the Community. Having given a proposal the next steps are as follows:

(a) the Commission gives notice to the parties concerned (i.e. Member State and recipient) to submit their comments;

(b) the Commission, in light of comments received, makes a finding of incompatibility, or compatibility or that the aid is being misused;

(c) the Commission will then take a formal decision requiring a Member State to abolish the aid or alter the aid within a set period of time;

(d) if the Member State fails to comply within the prescribed time, the Commission or any other interested State may refer the matter directly to the European Court of Justice.

Member States may apply to the Council for a decision permitting aid ruled incompatible by the Commission on the ground that exceptional circumstances obtained. If such special pleading is made to the Council, the Commission's procedure is suspended until the Council has made its attitude known.

Decisions by the Commission must be properly reasoned and have perspective effect only. Failure to comply with the time period prescribed in the Commission's decision by the Member State concerned empowers the Commission to commence Article 1169 proceedings before the Court of Justice. Alternatively Member States have two months after the decision of incompatibility to commence review proceedings under Article 173 of the Commission's decision.

4.10.5.1 PROCEDURE FOR NEW STATE AIDS

With regard to new aid, Article 93(3) lays down the procedure. Member states must inform the Commission of plans to grant new aid or alter existing aid. This must give the Commission sufficient time to enable it to submit its comments to the State concerned. If the Commission considers the aid to be incompatible with the Treaty then it must initiate the Article 93(2) procedure. Member States must suspend the grant of aid until Article 93(2) decision is given.

The obligation under Article 93(3) to notify aid is absolute. A failure to do so renders the aid incompatible.

The Court of Justice has set down a number of guidelines with regard to the Article 93(3) procedure. This can be summarised as follows:

(a) the preliminary stage for the procedure for reviewing aid under Article 93(3) is intended to enable the Commission to form a prima facie opinion. The suspension of the aid until the Commission has given its decision means that there is pressure on the Commission to form its opinion with expedition.

(b) the Court has indicated that the Commission has two months in which to undertake its prima facie assessment. The Member State may implement the aid after the expiry of the two month period if the Commission has failed to give a decision.

(c) if the Commission concludes its prima facie investigation positively, it must communicate that decision to the Member State concerned. The aid becomes existing aid and subject to the supervision rules of Article 93(1).

(d) if the Commission's prima facie view is negative, it must immediately initiate the full review procedure under Article 93(2).

(e) the initial investigation is made without comments from third parties. Therefore, the Commission must be convinced after the preliminary examination that the plan of aid is compatible with the Treaty. Otherwise it must move on to (d) above.

4.10.6 CONCLUSIONS ON STATE AID

Consequently, the rules on state aids have relevance in the sphere of environmental protection. It is submitted that a positive approach should be taken to state aid which is granted for the purposes of improving environmental protection. On the other hand, where state aid is granted to environmentally harmful projects, this should be one reason for ruling the aid incompatible not only with the competition rules but also with the general objectives of the Community.

V.

CONCLUSIONS

Chapter 5:

CONCLUSIONS

The purpose of this work has been to investigate the need for and possible models of interaction between competition law and environmental policy. The need stems largely from the same source as the adoption by the international community of the concept of sustainable development in Rio. In essence, industrial activity cannot forge on "willy nilly", ignoring the effects of its operations on the environment. Those effects should be investigated and where damage to the environment occurs or is anticipated, remedial or preventive action must be taken.

Competition laws when allied to welfare economics are a means by which the activities of companies are controlled so as to assist in an efficient allocation of the factors of production. Since the environment is now accepted as one of the factors of production either as a natural resource or as a receptacle for waste, competition rules can and should be used to affect the way in which companies use the environment. Agreements between companies with the purpose or effect of over-using their natural environment without internalizing the cost of so doing can be characterized as agreements which restrict competition since they will alter artificially the market conditions their competitors or potential competitors face. Similarly, agreements between competitors to enhance environmentally friendly technology may be seen to restrict competition but may be legitimated by the beneficial environmental consequences. Firms enjoying full or near monopoly power may be treated as abusing that power if they upset the market conditions by failing accurately to reflect the environmental costs of their activities. Indeed the ability to do so may in itself be an indication of dominance or monopoly power, the result of which is to expose the undertaking to greater scrutiny by the competition authorities and often stricter standards of competitive (and therefore environmentally friendly) behaviour. Finally, mergers between undertakings are seen as either beneficial or detrimental depending upon their effects on the concentration in the markets on which the participants operate. Crucial to this is the definition of the relevant market. As the environmental consequences of a product become more important in the eyes of the consumer, so drawing of markets by way of substitutes will change. Environmentally damaging goods will become increasingly less substitutable for "eco-products" with the effect that eco-industry is gradually developing to the detriment of traditional products. A merger between two firms, one manufacturing a traditional product and the other producing its "eco-counterpart" may be condoned on account of its possible extension of the "eco-technology" into old industries, de-concentrating the eco-market. Alternatively, where the concentrationn of a market as a result of a merger has the effect of entrenching the traditional product against the new eco-product, such a merger may be found to be anti-competitive on account of the deleterous consequences for the environment.

All the above are hypotheticals and this concluding Chapter is not the place for an exhaustive list of the ways and means by which competition rules can be used to serve the ends of environmental protection. Suffice it to say that free trade requires a level playing field in which traders operate. The level playing field in turn requires that comparative advantages are shifted naturally. As the international community becomes increasingly aware of the need to take environmental protection into account so it becomes necessary for production processes to internalize the environmental costs of manufacture and consumption. Otherwise, the comparative advantage becomes distorted and so in turn does the level playing field. Similarly, competition rules need to be consistent both in their content and application to avoid artificial barriers to trade and distortions in the level playing field.

Once the level playing field is established, so competition between undertakings can flourish with an accurate distribution of the factors of production resulting.

This work has studies three principal models in existing Treaties and Agreements to demonstrate the various stages of interaction of competition and environment. The first stage is the level playing field. The example used is GATT and the WTO. It was found that GATT has a long way to go to the establishment of a level playing field, but that moves are afoot to introduce environmental needs into the system. Unfortunately, the present framework is not based on a sound economic footing and therefore the playing field is distorted by the political aspirations of the contracting parties. Similarly there is no recognition of the effects of variable application of competition laws on the level playing field of trade which results in new and often hidden barriers being established. The consequence is that free trade interests continue to prevail with at present little regard paid to the consequences on the environment. Further the ways in which competition law can be used to protect environmental interests are reduced because of the inadequate system of exceptions from the GATT obligations for both environmental and competition rules.

The second model examined is NAFTA which appears on its face to go a step further in its contracting parties' commitment to environmental protection than the GATT. The system is, however, by no means perfect and is perhaps too novel to test effectively at present.

Of the three models investigated, the EC is the most progressive. Article 130r(2) EC requires Member States and Community institutions to integrate environmental policy into the defintion and implementation of all other policies of the EC including competition policy. Both the EC's environmental and competition policies have been developed in isolation from each other, the former largely through legislative measures and the latter through the caselaw of the Commission and the European Court of Justice in the application of the competition Articles in the Treaty, 85, 86, 90 and 92. The emphasis has however shifted in environmental policy to a more integrated approach requiring individuals and undertakings to take greater responsibility for the environment. This shift bolsters the suggestions in this book that, on the one hand, development of environmental law when harmonized throughout the Community will provide more opportunities for competition and in the long run will enable industrial activity to continue along the lines of the sustainable development model. On the other hand, the competition rules can be used to affect the ways in which undertakings in competition with each other interact so as to take into account the needs of environmental protection. Markets will be defined differently to separate out eco-products from their more traditional counterparts; research and development into eco-technology between competing firms can be seen as pro-competitive; specialized means of distribution such as selective distribution and franchising can be enhanced where the environmental consequences of a product in its sale, consumption and disposal so require; the behaviour of firms with monopoly power can be restricted when damage to the environment is threatened by characterizing such activity as an abuse of the dominant position; mergers between firms in the new eco-markets can be seen as pro-competitive whilst mergers between firms in dying traditional markets can be challenged on the basis that the former will be opening up new opporunities denying the merger parties market power over the long term whilst the latter can be seen as an attempt to entrench the old market against threats from eco-products and therefore anti-competitive.

At present, however, much of what has been suggested in the text is theoretical and hypothetical. The number of decisions embracing the integration rule in Article 130r(2) EC is paltry. Policy statements by the Council of Ministers, Commission and the European Parliament emit the right signals but these have not yet been put into practice. We must await the first challenge of an agreement through the competition rules on the basis that it is environmentally damaging or breaches the environmental policy of the EC and therefore is anti-competitive or restrictive of competition.

In summary, the need for interaction between competition law and environmental policy is clear and is implicit in the international community's adoption of sustainable development. However, as yet there is no working example of how this interaction is to operate. All we have are a number of theoretical examples in the neo-nascent stage.

The development of these models depends at the bottom line on political will, and here lies the rub. Taking the most progressive model as an example, the reluctance of the twelve Member States of the EC to apply environmental legislation is evident in the vast number of infringement actions brought against them by the Commission under Article 169 EC. Further, the institutional system in the EC works against the integration idea. There is little evidence of formal and adequate cross-communication between the various Directorates General in the Commission which implement EC legislation with the consequence that in competition decisions the bureaucrats (for want of a better word) have little expert knowledge of the environmental dimension of an agreement or market and therefore cannot be expected to comply with the integration rule in Article 130r(2) fully or adequately. Similarly, the environmental staff in DGXIII cannot be expected to have a full understanding of competition law, and therefore may not realize the opportunities available in Articles 85, 86, 90 and 92 to assist in the implementation of environmental policy.

It is not suggested that the interaction between competition law and environmental policy is the panacea for the threat facing the world's environment. Because competition law is directed at individual firms, it can never be a vehicle to combat for example damage done to the global commons. Nevertheless, it provides one weapon in the armoury against destruction of the environment. More needs to be done both to educate the international and domestic communities about the possibilities provided by the interaction to enhance both the environment and, through the use of environmentally friendly technologies, industrial activity. This book is not intended to provide answers, but it is hoped that it will have sparked off some interest and ideas to assist in the understanding of the need to protect and nurture our environment.

INDEX

A

Abuse of dominant position

competition, affecting *164-165*

environmental protection, affecting *180*

examples of *172-180*

joint *165*

jurisdiction over *165-166*

normal practice, consideration of *166*

predatory pricing *176-178*

Action Programmes, EC

First *83*

Second *84*

Third *84*

Fourth *85*

Fifth *12, 86-87*

Agreements restricting competition

automatically void *106*

de minimis principle and *110*

environmental protection and *103ff.*

horizontal *106*

minor importance *110*

trade associations, between *107*

vertical *110*

Article 30 EC

actions to which applicable *88-89*

Danish Bottles case *88, 156-157*

environmental policy *81, 156-157*

Walloon Import Ban case *88*
Article 36 EC
claims under *81*
Danish Bottles case
effect of *81, 156-157*
Walloon Import Ban case *88*
Article 85 EC
analysis of *104ff.*
Article 85(1), agreements to which applicable *106-107*
Article 86, relationship with *103-104*
automatically void agreements *106*
cooperation agreements, application to *106-107*
competition law, one of twin pillars *103*
coverage of *104ff.*
effects doctrine *111-114*
environmental policy, relationship with *93-103*
Merger Regulation, relationship with *181-182*
minor importance *110*
procedure *158-159*
trade associations *107*
trade between Member States *108-111*
undertakings within *108*
Article *86*
abuse see Abuse of dominant position
Article 85, relationship with *103-104*
competition law, one of twin pillars *103*
effects doctrine *170-174*
environmental protection, link with *180*
joint dominance, application to *165*

Merger Regulation, relationship with *181-182*

procedure *158-159*

see also Abuse of dominant position; dominance.

Article 90

purpose of *188-190*

see also Public undertakings

Assessment see Environmental assessment

B

Block exemptions see Regulations, exemption by

Brittan, Sir Leon *29, 31*

C

Cartels

common types of *107*

concerted practices, definition of *107*

Charging for pollution see Economic mechanisms for regulation

Clean-up

costs *25-29*

Common Market see European Community (EC)

Community law see European Community (EC)

Competition

advantages of *18-19, 90-104*

level playing field *22-24*

meaning *90, 113*

perfect *90*

trade law, relationship with *29-32*

workable, definition *93-97*

Competition law
European
environmental policy, relationship with *93-103*
future of *204-205*
integration theory *78-80*
origins of *73-78*
GATT, relationship with *11, 29-32*
level playing field *22-24*
NAFTA, relationship with *62*
procedure *158-159*
Competition policy
aims in framing *29-32, 90-93*
environmental policy, relationship with *32-34, 93-103*
integration theory *78-80*
international trade policies, relationship with *29-32*
Competition rules
de minimis principle *110*
environmental legislation, relationship to *93-97*
environmental policy, relationship to *97-103*
GATT, relationship to *29-32*
NAFTA, relationship to *62*
Council, EC see European Community (EC)
Court of First Instance (EC) *81*
Court of Justice (EC) *81*

D

Danish Bottles case *88*
Discrimination
GATT

most favoured nation principle *34*
national treatment principle *34*
Distribution
methods of *122-131*
selective, see Selective Distribution
Dominance
collective *165*
concept of *165*
definition *165*
eco-markets and *166-168*
factors of *168-170*
market share, with reference to *168*

E

Eco-industry *96-97*
Eco-labelling *135*
Eco-products *97-198*
Eco-rights *86-90*
Eco-technology *96*
Economic growth *10-13, 93*
Economic mechanisms for regulation
EC approach *83-86*
internalization of costs *24-25*
market mechanisms *85-86*
polluter pays principle see Polluter pays principle
state aids see State aids
subsidies *190*
Enforcement procedures

competition rules as *97*
nature of mechanisms *86*
Environment, definition *9*
Environmental assessment
EC Directive *16*

Environmental Impact Assessment see Environmental assessment
Environmental law
competition law and *78-80*
EC *79-83*
features *82-86*
international *8-11*
modern developments *10, 85-86*
regional, NAFTA *58-64*
Environmental rights
EC constitutional rights, as *86-90*
fundamental rights, as *87*
Environmental taxes see Economic mechanisms for regulation
Equity, intergenerational *9-10*
European Commission *73-74, 81*
European Community
Action Programmes see Action Programmes, EC
Council of Ministers *81*
environmental policy
Article 235 *82*
Article 100 and 100A *82*
Article 130r, 130s and 130t *80, 87*
competition law and *78-79*
constitutional basis *81-82*

future of *85-86*
integration into other policies *79-80*
institutions *81*
Single European Act *79*
Treaty on European Union see Treaty on European Union
European Parliament *81*
Exclusive dealing
block exemption *161*
Exclusive distribution agreements
Article 85(1), and *114*
block exemption *161*
Exclusive purchasing agreements
block exemption *161*

F

Foreclosure of market *171, 174-178*
Franchising
agreements *127*
Article 85 *127-131*
block exemption *161-162*
definition *127*
eco-products and *131*
know-how *127*
production *128*
varieties of *127-128*
Free trade
environmental policy, relationship with *11*
GATT *11, 32ff*

level playing field *11, 22-23*
NAFTA *53*

G

GATT
Agreement on Trade-related Intellectual Property Rights
Agreement on the Phytosanitary Measures *45*
competition policy, relationship with *29-32*
Decision on Trade & Environment *46*
economic approach *24*
environmental policy, relationship with *32-34*
environmental provisions of *32-43*
exceptions to obligations under *38-43*
history *23*
integration theory *23*
level playing field *11, 22*
Most favoured nation principle *34*
National treatment principle *34*
non-discrimination under *34*
procedure *47-49*
structure *22-24*
Uruguary Round of negotiations *31, 33, 51*
welfare economics in *22-23*
World Trade Organisation *22, 33, 49-51*
Geographical markets *166-168*
Government involvement
commercial activities *188-189*
competitive activity, eliminating *189*

public undertakings *103*

H

Human rights
environmental rights as *98-99*
European Convention on *98*

I

NATTA *64*
Integration theory
EC *78-80*
GATT *21-34, 49*
NAFTA *56-58*
Intellectual property rights
EC *78-80*
GATT *21-34, 49*
International environmental law
competition law, relationship with *8-10*
development of *8-10*
eco-rights *10*
generational rights *9-10*
treaty regimes *8-10*
UNEP *9*

J

Joint ventures

definition *118*
environmental purposes as justification of *119*
Merger Regulation (EC) and *183*
objective of *118*
research and development, for *118-119*

K

Know-how
eco-technology, as *163*
meaning *163*
Know-how licences
block exemption *163*
application of *163*
opposition procedure *163*
structure *163*

M

Maastricht Treaty see Treaty on European Union
Market sharing agreements *114-115*
Merger Regulation (EC)
Articles 85 and 86, relationship with *181-182, 182*
coming into effect *182*
competition issues, primarily concerned with 184,186-187
concentrations
assessment, criteria of *183*
compatibility with common market *184-187*
dominant position, creating or strengthening *184*

joint venture as *183*
meaning *183*
environmental policy and *184-187*
non-competition grounds as defence *184-187*

N

NAFTA
competition law and *55*
competition policy and *56-58*
environmental Articles of *58-62*
environmental scope of *11, 61-62*
member states of *11, 55*
purpose *55, 56*
side agreement on environment *62-71*

O

Organiztion of Economic Coperation and Development (OECD) *13*

P

Patent licences *162-163*
Patents
Articles 30-36 EC *119-121*
TRIPS *46*

Polluter pays principle
defintion *13-15*
Precautionary principle
definition *15-16*
foreseeability of harm *15-16*
Pricing
discounts and rebates *115-116*
discriminatory *115-116*
environmental cost, internalization of *24-25*
excessive *172, 178-179*
predatory *176*
Product market *166-167*
Public undertakings
competition rules and *104*
conduct of *104*
environmental rules and *104*

R

Rebates
abuse of dominant position *176-177*
environmental *176-177*
Refusal to supply *179*
Regulation 17/62 (EC) *73-74*
Regulations (EC), exemption by category
distribution, exclusive *161*
franchising *161-162*
licensing
know-how *163*

patent *162-163*
research and development *163-164*
Relevant market
geographic,
concept of under Article 86 *166-167*
product
concept of under Article 86 *166-167*
definition of in Article 86 *166*
Research and development agreements *163-164*
Restructuring
joint research and development and *163-164*
joint ventures and *118*
Rule of reason *105*

S

Sanctions
EC law and *106*
GATT and *47-49*
NAFTA *65-69*
Regulation 17/62 *73-74*
Selective distribution agreements
customer limitation clauses in *122-123*
environmental considerations in *124-127*
exclusive purchasing in *124*
Settlement
EC Commission, with *158-159*
Single European Act
amendments by *79*

State aid
definition *191-192*
environmental considerations in *192-196, 198*
sanctions *196-198*
State behaviour *188-200*
State interference, competition and
competition, restriction of *188-189*
competition rules, infringement of *189*
responsibility not to assist *189*
responsibility not to encourage *189*
State monopoly *104*
Stocking requirements
distribution agreements in *126*

T

Technical development *9-10, 12-13, 76-78*
Technical progress
definition *88*
environmental progress as *139-141*
safety standards as *138-139*
"Towards Sustainability" see Action Programmes (EC)
Treaty on European Union
environmental provisions of *79*
integration theory in *78-80*
Trade associations *107*
Trade, Member States between
appreciability *108-109*
concept of *108-109*

national cartels *107*
Trademark agreements
EC *112-121*
GATT *46*
TRIPS *46*
Turnover
de minimis principle and *108-109*
Merger Regulation (EC) *182*

U

Undertakings
association of *108*
definition *182*
Unfair pricing *172, 178-179*
United Nations Conference on Environment and Development *10, 15*
United Nations Conference on the Law of the Sea (UNCLOS III)*17*
15
United Nations Environmental Programme *9*

W

Waste disposal *18*
Water
international conventions *15, 17*
Water Act 1989 *169*
Water Industry Act 1991 *169*

CASES

ECJ

AEG Telefunken v. Commission Case 107/82 [1983] ECR 3151 *105*

BAT v. Commission (Phillip Morris)Cases 142 & 156/84 [1988 4 CMLR 24 *180*

Bayerische HNL Vermehungsbetriebe v. Commission Case 83/46 [1978] 3CMLR 565 *90*

Belasco v. Commission Case 246/86 [1989] ECR 2128 *105*

Benedetti v. Minari Case 52/76 [1977] ECR 163 *191*

Biovilac S.A. v. Commission Case 59/83 [1977] 2 CMLR 881 *91*

BNIC v. Clair Case 123/83 [1985] ECR 392 *187*

BP v. Commission Case 77/77 [1978] ECR 1513 *171*

Brasserie De Haecht v. Wilkin (No.1) Case 23/67 [1967] ECR 407 *109*

BRT v. Sabam (1) [1974] ECR 51 *130*

Centrafarm v. Winthrop BV Case 16/74 [1934] ECR 1183 *106*

Commercial Solvents v. Commission Case 6 & 7/73 [1974] ECR 223 *178, 179*

Commission v. Belgium Case C-2/90 Waloon Waste Import Ban *17, 87, 166*

Commission v. Germany Case 248/83 [1985] ECR 1459 *99*

Commission v. France Case 290/83 [1985] ECR 493 *191*

Commission v. Denmark Case 302/86 Danish Beer Bottles [1988] ECR 4607 *87, 156*

Consten SA and Grundig - Verkaufs GmbH v. Commission Cases 56 & 58/64 [1966] ECR 299 *104, 108, 119, 133, 136*

Defrenne v. Sabena (2) Case 149/177 [1978] ECR 1365 *101*

Defrenne v. Sabena Case 43/76 [1976] ECR 454 *101*

Dekker v. VJV-Centrum Case 177/88 [1990] ECR 3841 *100*

Delimitis v. Henninger Brau AG Case 234/89 *109*

Enichem v. Cinisello Balsamo Case 380/87 [1969] ECR 2491 *93*

Eridania v. Ministry of Agriculture Case 230/78 [1979] ECR 2749 *91*

Europemballage & Continental Can v. Commission Case 6/72 [1973] ECR 215 *165, 173, 174*

FRUBO Case 71/74 [1975] ECR 563 *106*

General Motors Continental v. Commission Case 26/75 [1975] ECR 1367 *177*

Greek Television Eiliniki Radiophonia Tileorassi v. Dimotiki Etairi Pliroforissi Case C-260/89 [1992] ECR I-2925 *98*

Hartz v. Aldi Case 179/88 [1990] ECR 3879 *100*

Hauer v. Land Rineland-Pfalz Case 44/79 [1980] 3 CMLR 42 *90*

Hoffman-la-Roche v. Commission, Vitamins Case 85/76 ECR 461 *172, 182*

ICI v. Commission Case 48/49 [1972] ECR 619 *106*

Johnston v. RUC Case 222/84 [1986] ECR 1651 *100*

L'Oreal v. Nieuwe AMCK Case 31/80 [1980] ECR 3775 *123*

Leclerc v. Au Blé Vert Case 229/83 [1985] ECR 11 *87*

Metro v. Commission (1) Case 26/76 [1976] ECR 1875 *122, 123, 124*

Michelin v. Commission Case 332/81 ECR 3461 *167, 182*

Miller Schallplatter v. Commission Case 19/77 [1978] ECR131 *111, 113*

Nold v. Commission Case 4/73 [1974] 2 CMLR 338 *91*

Pronuptian v. Irmgrad Schillgalis [1986] ECR 353 *127, 128, 129*

Society for the Protection of the Unborn Child (Ireland) Ltd. v. Grogan et al Case 159/80 [1991] 3 CMLR 849 *97*

Steenkolennijnen v. High Authority Case 30/59 [1971] ECR 1 *190*

Stremsel v. Commision Case 61/80 [1981] ECR 851 *107*

Suiker Unie v. Commission, Sugar Cases 40 etc./73 [1976] 1 CMLR 295 *172*

Telemarketing Case 311/84 [1985] ECR 3261 *177*

Tetrapak Rausing v. Commission Case T-51/89 [1992] 4 CMLR 334 *174*

United Brands v. Commission Case 26/76 [1978] ECR 207 *167, 177*

Vereeniging Von Cementhandelaren v. Commission Case 8/72 [1972] ECR 977 *106, 108*

Vlaamse Reisbureaus v. ZW Case 311/85 [1987] ECR 3801 *7 8 , 188*

Volk Vervaecke Case 5-69 [1969] ECR295 *109*

Wachauf Case 5/88 [1989] ECR 2609

EC Commission

ACEC Berler [1968] CMLR D35 *153*

Aerospatiale - Aliena De Haviland Case IV/MO53 [1991] L334/42 *185, 186*

AKZO OJ [1985 L374/1 *170, 176*

Amersham / Buchler [1983] 1 CMLR 619 *142, 120*

Ansac OJ [1991] L152/54 *148*

Assurpol [1993] 4 CMLR 338 *146, 153*

Bayer / Gist-Brocades [1976] 1 CMLR D98 *142, 143*

Bayer AG OJ [1990] L21/7 *117*

BBC Brown Boveri / NGK [1989] CMLR 610 *118,145,149,153*

BMW OJ [1975] L29/1 *138, 139*

Boosey & Hawkes OJ [1987] L286/36 *170*

BP/Kellogg [1986] 2 CMLR 619 *118*

BPB Industries & British Gypsum OJ [1989] L10/50 *170*

British Sugar OJ [1988] L284/41 *170*

Carbon Gas Technology [1985] 2 CMLR 275 *134*

Computerland [1988] 4 CMLR 259 *127*

Continental Can [1972] CMLR D11 *164*

Costen & Grundig [1964] CMLR 489 *155*

D'Ieteren Motor Oils OJ [1991] L 20/42 *125*

Hilti OJ [1988] L65/19 *170*

IBM [1984] 2 CMLR 342 *125, 126*

International Energy Agency [1984] 2CMLR 186 *144, 149*

Italian Flat Glass [1990] 4 CMLR 535 *164*

Junghans [1977] 1 CMLR D82 *125*

KEWA [1976] 2 CMLR D15 *150*

KSB / Lowara / Goulds Pumps / IT OJ [1990] L19/25 *153, 159*

Magill TV guide OJ [1989] L78143 *170*

Mitchell Cotts / Sofiltra [1988] 4 CMLR 111 *118*

Navewa - Anseau [1982] 2 CMLR 193 *111*

Optical Fibres OJ [1988] L235/30 *118*

Sabena OJ [1988] L317/47 *170*

Synthetic Fibres [1985] 1 CMLR 787 *152*

Tetrapak OJ [1988] L272/27 *170*

United Reprocessors GmbH [1976] 2 CMLR D1 *139,141,142,149, 157*

Villeroy & Boch [1988] 4 CMLR 461 *125*

VOTOB Commission 22nd Report on Competition Policy, para. 177 *147, 153, 155*

Yves Rocher [1988] 4 CMLR 592 *127, 129*

Yves St. Laurent Perfumes OJ [1992] L 12/24 *133*

International

Cosmos 954 [1979] 18 ILM 902 *16*

GATT Panel Report US - Restrictions on Imports of Tuna (1991) 30 ILN 1598. *85*

GATT Panel Report Thailand - Restriction on Importation of and Taxes from Cigarettes, BISD 37S *170*

Measures Affecting Exports of Unprocessed Herring & Salmon O/ 6268, 35 BISD. *41*

Trail Smelter [1939] 33 AJ1L 182 *84*

LEGISLATION

12th Report on Competition Policy (EC). *189*

17th Report on Competition Policy (EC). *194*

1st Environmental Action Programme (EC) OJ [1973] C112. *82*

2nd Environmental Action Programme (EC) OJ [1977] C139. *83*

3rd Environmental Action Programme (EC) OJ [1983] C46. *83*

4th Environmental Action Programme (EC) *83*

5th Environmental Action Programme (EC) OJ [1993] C138. *74, 75, 81, 84, 95, 117, 187*

Brussels Convention on Civil Liability for Oil Pollution Damage, 1984 Protocol. *16*

CITES [1973] 993 UNTS 243 *55*

Clayton Act (USA). *21*

Commission Memorandum on Problem of Industrial Concentration in Common Market, Competition Series No.31 *80*

Commission Communications on Industrial Competitiveness and Environmental Protection (SEC (1992) 1986 Final). *149*

Commission - 1st Report on Competition Policy (EC) (1971). *188*

Community Charter of Fundamental Social Rights (EC) Art. 8. *99*

Competition Act 1980 (UK). *21*

Convention for the Regulations of Antarctic Mineral Resources Activities - Art. 4. *14*

Convention for the Regulation of Antarctic Mineral Resource Activities 1988 *16*

Council Directive 76/548 (EC) OJ [1967] L196. *81*

Council Resolution (EC) OJ [1992] C331/5. *96*

Directive 76/207 (EC), Art.2(2). *99, 100*

Directive 85/337/EEC on Environmental Impact Assessment (EC) OJ [1985] L175/40. *14, 15*

EC Treaty, Arts:

2 *80, 81, 100, 184*

3(f) *174*

3(g) *77, 89, 102*

3(i) *71*

3(n) *77*

5 *187*

30 *87*

36 *80, 155*

42 *96*

56 *98*

59 *98*

74 *96*

84 *77, 78, 89, 97, 102, 103-109, 164, 169, 170, 183, 187, 188, 191 193*

86 *77, 78, 89, 97, 102, 103, 163-180, 182, 187, 191*

87 *77, 181*

88 *77, 181*

89 *77, 181*

90 *77, 103*

91 *77*

92 *77, 89, 103, 189, 190, 191, 192, 193*

93 *77, 189, 195, 197*

94 *77*

95 *77*

100 *81*

119 *99*

130a *184*

130r *78, 86, 87, 132, 138, 145, 147,150, 156, 157, 158, 159, 160, 175, 179, 180, 185, 186, 188, 189, 194, 202, 203*

130s *78*

130t *78*

155 *80*

169 *73, 93, 94, 187, 203*

170 *94*

171 *94*

173 *196*

189 *93*

215 *91*

222 *118*

223 *96*

232 *96*

235 *81*

Eco-Labelling Scheme, Council Regulation 880/92 (EC) OJ [1992] L99/1. *152*

Environmental Protection Act s.59 (UK). *168*

Environmental Protection Act 1990 (UK). *168*

European Convention on Human Rights. *86*

European Convention on Human Rights - Protocol No.1. *190*

Exclusive Purchasing Regulation (EC) 1984/83. *159*

Exclusive Distribution Regulation (EC) 1983/83. *159, 160*

Franchising Regulation (EC) 4087/88. *159, 160*

GATT, Arts:

I *33*

II *33*

III *33*

VI *34*

X *35*

XI *35*

XVI *36*

XVIII *37*

XX *37, 58, 61*

XXII *46*

XXIII *46*

GATT Agreement on Trade Related Intellectual Property Rights *45*

GATT Agreement on Technical Barriers to Trade (1979 version) *22*

GATT Agreement on Technical Barriers to Trade (1994 version) *23, 43*

GATT Decision on Trade and Environment *45*

GATT Agreement on Sanitary and Phytosanitary Measures *44*

Health & Safety at Work Act 1974 s.3 (UK). *168*

International Salvage Convention 1989 *16*

Know How Licensing, Regulation 556/89 (EC). *159, 162*

London Dumping Convention. *15*

Management Quality Assurance EN ISO 9000 1994 (Formerly BS5750). *85*

Merger Regulation (EC) 4064/89, Arts:

2 *183, 184, 185*

3 *182*

5 *181*

22 *181*

Montreal Protocol on Substances that Deplete the Ozone Layer (1987) 26 KM 1550. *55*

NAFTA, Arts:

104 *58*

114. *60*

904(2), *59*

905(1) *59*

907(2). *59*

1106. *61*

NAFTA Side Agreement, Arts:-

1 *62*

3 *63*

5 *64*

6 *64*

7 *65*

9 *63, 70*

11 *68*

14 *69*

15 *69*

20 *68*

23 *66*

24 *67*

45 *66*

Annex 34 *67*

Patent Licensing, Regulation 2349/84 (EC). *159, 161*

R & D Regulation 418/85 (EC) OJ [1985] L53/5. *117, 159, 163*

Implementing Regulation (MR) 2356/90 (EC) *186*

Regulation 17 of 1962 (EC). *73, 103, 181*

Restrictive Trade Practices Act 1976 (UK). *21*
Treaty on European Union Art. F. *85*
UNCLOS 1982 Arts:
139. *16*
206. *14*
235. *16*
Water Industry Act 1991 s.118, s.210 (UK). *168*
Water Act 1989 (UK). *168*